the blue of every flame

the blue of every flame

ryan quinn flanagan

INTERIOR NOISE PRESS
Cleveland, OH

The Blue of Every Flame
Copyright © 2015 by Ryan Quinn Flanagan

All rights reserved. No part of this book may be used or reproduced in any manner whatsoever without written permission except in the case of brief quotations embodied in critical articles and reviews.

For order information and current mailing address please visit www.interiornoisepress.com

Interior Noise Press
Cleveland, OH

Cover Photograph by Shona Helen Hardy
Book Design by David p Bates

ISBN: 978-0-9961093-0-7

First Edition

For femsly

contents

Urinating on a Police Cruiser in the First Person	15
Sudbury	16
Bloodletting in the 21st Century	17
Molly Once Removed	18
The Blue of Every Flame	19
Kicking my Grandfather into Oblivion	20
Moses Below Sea Level	21
Say Cheese	22
88A	23
Christ On the Lawn	24
Queensway Books	25
Deconstructionist Art is a Messy Affair	26
Skipping Rosetta Stones Across the Backs of the Ages	27
Who Needs An Iceberg?	28
Confessions of an Asshole, in the First Person	29
For Freedom or Democracy or Something	30
Mary's a Grand Old Name	31
A Sense of Style is What Separates Genius from Jumpers	32
Gloria	33
Throat Banging for Beginners/The Spectre of Laughter	34
Spandex and Issues	35
The Woman Who Works Lingerie	36
Redneck Ant Farm	37
The Young Republicans	38
Looking for Lovers?	39
The Bottom Line	41
Bonnie and Clyde	42
Death of a Motivational Speaker	44
Shoplifter	45
The Fall	47
Heavy Wet Pulse of the Inner Harbour at Night	48
Rivers	49
Heaven is a Toothbrush with Most of the Bristles Missing	51
A Word of Advice	52
Bon Appetit	53
Brownnoser	54
Chivalry is Dead as a Dried Bunk Sock Under the Bed	55
Dreams of Marilyn	56
Fair Trade	57

For Every Dick There is a Richard	58
Happy Face	59
His Luck	60
I'm Here to Tell You...	61
Keeping the Minutes	62
Liquid Buddha of the Faded Inkblot Sun	64
MAD	66
Murphy Bed	67
New Sink	68
POW	69
Safe Words	70
Slavery is Too Much from Too Little Just as it has Always Been	71
Southern Love	72
Tent City	73
The Magician	74
Wood and Silence	75
Speed Demon	76
Love is a Motherfucker	77
Genocide is Cruel, Your Friends can be Even Crueler	78
Yet Another Fine Coming of Age Story	79
Children	80
I'm Confused	81
The Calendar on the Wall Well Hung	82
The Reading	83
The Rape of Baseboard Heaters in Something Revealing	84
Treadmills Are an Ingenious Way for Rats in Traffic to Stay Fit	85
Kid on a Stick	86
24 hr. Kinkos	87
The Shoplifters of Singapore	89
If Only Animals Looked Half as Good as they Taste	90
A Smart Business Decision	91
Not Death, Just Taxes	92
Some Men Get Less for Murder	93
Mean Muggin' the Baby Jesus	94
Something to Remember	95
First Love	96
Vlad the Inhaler	97

Girl in the Park	98
A Freezer Full of Bovine Ejaculate, in the Month of Taurus	99
Between Cinder Blocks the Mad Heart Plays	100
Toaster Ovens are Hot, but this was Different	101
Bedtime Stories of the Damned	102
2 Razors	103
oh Nietzsche!	104
Lighter Fluid Skin Melting Away like a Cheese Fondue	105
The Girls from the Colonial Style Bordello	106
A Million Laughs that No One Else Ever Seems to Hear	108
The Little Arm That Could	109
Rocket Attack	110
Brazilian	111
While the Fingernail Pullers of Iran Share Tea	113
For Your Viewing Pleasure	114
Dumpster Dive	115
Sad, the Same Way Clearance Sales Are Sad	116
This is What Got the Hindenburg	117
Beluga Joe	118
Meth Lab	119
Aerial Bombardment	120
Tall Order	121
They Took Him Away	122
Buskers' Week	123
Man is a Social Network	125
C is NOT for Cookie	126
Kush Monster	127
The Bomb is Just Something they Hold Over Your Head, like Rainbows	128
Ass Slinky	129
I Wish I was Charles	130
Curled Hair That Wants to be the Number Six	131
Rust Proofing Your Urethra	132
Hank Williams	133
Carwash	135
Martha's Table	142
On the Mend	143
Khmer Rouge Does Not Make You Look Pretty	144
A Little Bit Country	145

New Canadian	146
Prince Albert	147
Water Board a Gerbil, and You Still Have Disagreement	148
Soda Fountain Stuck	149
His Arm Was Broken	150
Puppy Mill	151
A Speaker from the School of Divinities	152
Modern Art, All Over the Back of the Toilet Bowl	153
Forced Eviction	154
I Can Do Anything a MAN Can	155
Latter Day Ain'ts	156
I'm Not Worried	157
A Good Company Man	158
Everything Must Go	159
Like Your Very Own Pretty Little Hiroshima	160
Windows Are Transparent, Governments Are Not	161
Army Brat	162
Delish	164
Getting Cheeky	165
Tchaikovsky was a Fruit, and so Are Pineapples	166
The Seven Year Old Psychic	167
Ode to GG Allin, I Guess	168
Food Court	169
Boots on the Ground	170
Volunteer Firefighters	172
Isaac Newton Proved Right Yet Again	173
Day Labourer	174
The Drunken Church Sign Alteration	175
Meals on Wheels	177
Why a New York Times Bestseller Will Never Be Anyone That Matters	178
Urine Pucks	179
Drive-By	180
Kiss the Cook	181
Pilot Project	182
Zero Sum	183
Death Never Happened on a Waterbed	184
Fear Keeps Many People in Work	185
sometimes	186

Running the Mouth, and Not the Generator	187
Punching my Ticket to Sainthood	189
Another Postition	190
Tea Kettle Madness	191
Finger Fuck a Hand Grenade, Things Get Messy	192
A Coney Island of the Dogs	193
The Talk	194
Jamaican Shower Posses	195
The Mob Puts Bodies Here but You Never See Them	196
Impeaching my Local Cable Service Provider	197
"Goodbye Everybody"	198
To the Left of Nowhere	199
Walmart Greeter	201
Bobbing for Apples, Well Into Adulthood	203
Yellow Cake Uranium Birthdays	204
A Moment in the Sun	205
Genius is Sticking a Grapefruit Down Your Pants and Realizing that is One Less Grapefruit the Starving World Wants to Eat	207
The Tongue Wresters of Modern France	208
That Million Dollar Idea is Only a Million Dollars Away	209
French River Trading Post	210
How Come Faith Healer Never Comes Up in the Want Ads?	212
Kingston Meats	213
Voted Most Likely to Succeed	214
She Says I'm a Difficult Man to Live With, and There May be Something to That	215
Money Only Knows	216
A Tree with Bark	217
Kickers Are People Too	218
Confessional	220
Tiny Sunsets	221
Haunted Walk	222
SURPRISE!	223
On a Three Day Greyhound Back Across the Country with Four Rows of Stale Cookies and a Whole New Outlook On Life	224
Zzzzzzzzzzzzzs	225
Get Bent	226

Student Painters	227
Nudist Colony	228
Bitch Be Cray Cray	229
Genius	231
Parking Enforcement	232
I Taste the Tongues that Rape Me	233
Communication Breakdown	234
Personal Touch	236
Rubber Brown Curtains	237
Get Help, Not Food	239
Two Queens	240
Controlled Burn	241
Day Pass Diva	242
Summer High Season	243
Topless Beach	244
Desperation is a Full Tank of Wanting	245
California Roll	246
Strangling Parrots, Choking Chickens	247
First Day of School	248
Even the Strippers Making Change	249
They Always like to Ask if You Are a Threat to the Community, but Never if the Community is a Threat to You	250
Fallout	251
Banana Boat Princess	252
Real Estate is at a Premium	253
Dinosaurs Are Extinct, and So Were We	254
For Another Minimum Wager	255
My Disarming Believable 5.75/hr Phone Voice	256
Fashion Week	259
References	260
Memory is a Bitch	261
His Rusted Out $200/as is Baby	262
Girls' Softball	264
Spiral Notebook	265
Empty Nester	266
Crabs	267
Short, Bald, and Ugly	268
With Mother's Day Just Around the Corner	269

Blue Wall of Sound	271
Much Trouble Breathing	272
Brand Loyalty	273
Gentlemen Prefer Blondes that Swallow	275
Winter Doughnuts	276
Grunt	278
Stand Up	279
Last Call	280
Sworn into Office, Now Swearing Under Oath	281
Bar Crawl	282
Ode to Herbert Spencer	283
Twin Pit Bulls	284
Disaster Movie Narcissism	285
Stretch Marks Are Just Storylines that Carry On Too Long	286
There Was a Man	287
Forget Poverty, I Want to Know About the Nose Hairs of the Dinosaurs	289
I Have Found	290
The Future Needs Rent Money and the Cost of Diapers Just like the Past	291
Free Ride	292
A Bend in the Road is Worth Two by the Mistress	293
My Week Beats Your Year	294
Another 40 Year Man Goes the Way of Big Tobacco	296
Bairros Africanos	297
Tow Trucks	298
Away Team	299
Bailiff	300
Paris in the Spring	301
Amen	302
Violence as a First Language	304
Slag	306
Secret Santa	311
217 Times	312
Patio Crowd	314
They Are	315
Slow Cookers Are Only for Those with Time	317
Easy as Pie	318

The most powerful weapon on earth is the human soul on fire.

FERDINAND FOCH

Urinating on a Police Cruiser in the First Person

After we polished off the vodka
and tipped mail boxes
to officially commit a federal offence,
we used the screwdrivers
we'd lifted from my father's tool box
to switch the license plates of a police cruiser
with a minivan in a driveway
a few houses up the street.

When the porch light came on
and the cop
in his housecoat leveled his gun,
all my friends
had scattered into the night
leaving only I
halfway through a good piss
on the driver's side door of the police cruiser.

The cop chased me away
before I had time to finish
and I ran through the streets
like an escaped fire hose,
leaving a sporadic trail
that wound across the pavement

and lead halfway home.

Sudbury

In room 202
of the Travelway Inn
on Paris Street
I woke up and knew
I had to eat something
or be sick.

I threw on some clothes
from the floor
and grabbed some change
off the side table.

Staggered two blocks West
to the nearest convenience store
and as I passed through the parking lot
I noticed a parked red Sonata
with half a face blown off
in the driver's seat.
The morning frost ensured that bits of cranium
caked frozen to part
of the driver's side window
after having slid down halfway.

I went into the convenience store
and bought a bag of pork rinds
and a Hustler.

I opened the bag
and ate one
as a crowd gathered around the car.

When I got back to my room
I pulled down the shades
folded my half eaten bag of pork rinds
to seal in freshness
and jerked off to the schoolgirl
and the charge nurse
doubled up
on page 24.

Bloodletting in the 21st Century

The horns of Harlem
filter down the twilight avenues
past the dogs
and bums
and urine trails that wind around the city
like an empty bladder womb.
The pimps
and tricks
mix with creamy Motown licks
as the sewer grate steam
of snare drum madness
explodes on the faces of the night.

A toothless old bass man
from Chicago
lets his fingers climb into the mind
of the city

while half a block away
in a second floor dive
I polish off a pack of smokes
to early Coltrane

and cut myself shaving.

Molly Once Removed

The leopard print
that just finished her three song set
to Blondie
sits beside me
and asks for a beer.

I tell her I know
her upstairs neighbour
and that she has two kids
that never stop crying.

I also tell her she's getting ripped off
by the ounce
has a stretch mark on her left thigh
even the fog machine can't hide
and that her show would be flawless
if she hugged the pole

a little tighter.

She calls me a freak
and moves onto
the next.

A geriatric
with a foley catheter
and a thick wad
of cash.

The Blue of Every Flame

Tweekers in car parks
jack cars for a fix
while muggers lay in wait
for first dates
and the Bowery drunks
stumble out into traffic
giving Happy Hour legs.

The black eyed susan across the hall
started tricking again
and now her old man
is back downtown
for assault and battery

while I sit half mad
on a bed full of empty Vodka minis
rubbing magazine cologne samples
all over my chest
and dancing in front of the vanity
like some dime store whirling dervish

as the roaches scurry
the neon hums
and the serviced johns in the stairwell
moan through paper thin walls.

All around me,
the world is alive

and I
am the mad manic heart
of the universe.

The blue of every flame.

Kicking my Grandfather into Oblivion

The chain link fence had keeled over
the same way my grandfather
had keeled over
and now there were some kids
kicking it
and standing on it
trying to bring it down
for good.
And I did not want them standing there
like that
laughing as they kicked my grandfather
into oblivion.
I grabbed a stick
and chased the kids away
and tried to restore my grandfather
to his former glory,
but the years
and wives
and laughing children
had not been
kind.

Across the street
a small crowd gathered
to watch a grown man weep
over a chain link fence doubled over
behind him.

With head in hands
on a curb
of concrete

and
sun.

Moses Below Sea Level

Moses below sea level
is just some guy
selling rocks.

Until recently,
he worked the southbound corner
at Duke and Lexington,
but since the buskers came to town
for a week of music
and styrofoam
he's moved uptown three blocks
with his change purse
patchy dog
and painted rocks.

The rocks don't move as well
uptown
but the dog eats better
and the free showers
and coffee
at the Lombardi Street Mission
are now

just minutes away.

A barber even works his part
once a month

below sea level.

Say Cheese

Some guy was stabbed in Queens
last night
trying to aid a woman
being attacked by a mugger
and as he lay dying on the sidewalk
his fellow citizens walked by
for more then an hour;
even the woman he had aided
ran off
and neglected to call
the cops.

A few onlookers rolled the dying man over
to see if he had a wallet
and one pedestrian stopped to snap
a picture
on his camera
phone.

An hour and 45 minutes later
paramedics arrived on the scene,
but it was too late.

Now,
that's one less guy
you'll have to stand behind
in the buffet line.

There are never enough plates
anyway.

88A

There was always one light on
each night
as I stumbled home
from the bar.

The rest of the lights on the street
were out
but the senile widow at 88A
always left her light on,
convinced that her husband who had been dead
five years
was cheating on her.

She was up at dawn each following morning
accosting passers by
and asking them
if they had seen her husband
who hadn't come home
last night.

One day
a white unmarked van came
and took her away
and a young family of first time homeowners
moved in.

Last night
the entire street was dark
when I stumbled home
from the bar.

Its been that way
for weeks now.

Christ On the Lawn

A mob gathered outside
my front window and
beat the shit out of
a dealer they said was
getting their kids hooked
on dangerous stuff.

At first
I thought about intervening
on the dealer's behalf
but I had things to do.

The mob passed judgement with sticks
and I
decided to let them use my lawn
while I grabbed a fresh beer
from the fridge
filled the dish sink with soap and
washed my hands of
the whole affair.

Two weeks later
the lawn across the street
was littered with pink flamingos
but
the mob
left them alone.

Queensway Books

The used bookstore near my apartment
is run by an old couple
who have lived above the store
for the last thirty-two years.
The old guy is scatterbrained
when it comes to anything other than his books
but ask him if he has some obscure
literary offering
by any near-unknown
and he will know exactly where it is.
Tens of thousands of books
just piled on the floor
in no discernible order,
but the old guy
seems to have a working catalogue
in his head.

The harlequins are in the front window.

The good stuff
is in the back.

If you're looking for something
in particular,
you'll have to ask.

The old guy seems to enjoy
talking to customers.

He no longer talks
to his wife.

She watches soaps
on a small 14" black and white
at the cash.
Barely looking away
to make change.

Deconstructionist Art is a Messy Affair

A pack of dogs
tore a small boy
to pieces
after he fell into the enclosure
on my way
to the store.

By the time
I came home
there was nothing
left.

And I unwrapped my chocolate bar
and thought
about that.

Skipping Rosetta Stones Across the Backs of the Ages

The dancing bear does circus tricks,
piñatas on the cover of S&M Monthly,

and my days are filled with little more
than laying here
staring at the ceiling
waiting for the muse to arrive
with the fire.
Skipping Rosetta stones across
the backs of the ages.
There are large craters in the couch upholstery
from where the heels of my idleness
have come to rest for far too long.
I run my hands across the contours
of another wasted moon landing

and wait
for it to get dark.

The dancing bear mauls a midget,
shadows dance across my walls;

sometimes a foxtrot
never a waltz.

Who Needs An Iceberg?

There is little I enjoy more in this world
than heading down to the local payphone
the junkies use to score
each night
and pretend to be making an important call
while the junkies fidget
and begin to shake.

I recently started wearing ear plugs
to block out the hours
of dial tone

but the junkies don't seem to notice.

You think they'd find another payphone
but junkies are the ultimate
creatures of habit.
They stick to their dealers
and payphones
like barnacles to the bottom
of a sinking ship.

A legion of hungry track marks

punching holes
in the Titanic.

Confessions of an Asshole, in the First Person

You know something has gone awry
when you drive around in a vehicle that has seats
that warm themselves
and a device over the rear view mirror
that gives you weather updates

to the second.

Eight dollar soy beads
that add to the smell of your candles
and a $37 water bowl that circulates
cat water

are the clincher.

Before long I'll have my hand woven underwear
imported from a Belgian nunnery
and refuse to sleep on anything but endangered duck throws
with blood diamond embossing.

Somewhere along the way
it all went wrong.

I remember a time in the not so distant past
when I slept in the snow
and fought off raccoons to keep the sandwich in my pocket.
Now, I have alternating towels
for different parts of the body,
and a Mexican that does my dishes
three times a day.

Sure I still wipe my own ass
but I could find someone

for that.

For Freedom or Democracy or Something

After basic in Borden
the soldiers congregate in Fred Grant Square
for a send off
before being shipped out to Halifax harbour
for deployment.

With each major deployment,
the municipal authorities
bring out the decorated veteran amputees
of the last war
to show off their shiny medals
as they limp
and wheel down main street.

The glares of both the veterans and
the soldiers are filled with contempt
when they look at unmarried men
of draft age
ignoring the festivities and
going about their daily business.

The soldiers say they are fighting
to defend me
but given the chance
they would kill me in a second.

Thankfully
they've found someone else to kill
half a world away
while I buy my carton of milk and
check out the girl at *Crossovers*
they say can shoot ping pong balls
out of her cunt.

Mary's a Grand Old Name

The brunette on the bed
who thinks I kinda look like James Cagney
says I can call her anything I want
but says her street name
is Mary

and a tiny smile betrays her hard veneer
as she loosens her garter
and I tell her
Mary is the preferred name of writers
religions
and royalty.

When she leaves
with the money off the dresser
I light a smoke
and listen to her heels clunk away down the hall
mumbling *Mary* to myself
each time she makes contact
with treated wood.

Outside,
the skies open up
and the backed up sewer drains
smell of rotten eggs.

A Sense of Style is What Separates Genius from Jumpers

There is a picture by I. Russell Sorgi of
a thirty-five-year-old divorcee in mid-jump as
she plunges from an eighth storey window ledge of
the Genesee Hotel in Buffalo
in 1942.
I have always been fascinated by
the woman's choice of a hotel ledge
when checking out.
I am far from certain the statement is deliberate but
the chance that it is makes me
adore her sense of irony.

I had the print blown up and
placed on my living room wall to
remind me that
you must always act with
an overpowering sense of

style.

Gloria

When Gloria got home from work
I took her by the hand
and told her
that a plane would be flying overhead at seven
and that
she might want to change into
something nice.

The largest smile came over her face
as she skipped away down the hall
toward the bedroom
and when she emerged
she had on her tight red dress
which she only wore
on special occasions.

We gathered on the front lawn
by seven
and a few moments after
a single engine Cessna flew by
with a banner in tow
that read clear as day:

Oswald Was Not The Only Shooter

Without a word
she let go of my hand
and went inside.

She seemed disappointed
that Oswald was not the only shooter.

She was even more dissatisfied
when the bill for the plane came
and she found out

I had used her credit card.

Throat Banging for Beginners/The Spectre of Laughter

The boys with long fingernails
aren't getting any action
just as every shining little boner
makes you really put your back
into it
and the unemployment line
never gets shorter.

And I feel like checking my salad
for grammar
while the $10 mouth gives throat banging lessons
for beginners
out in the back alley

and the spectre of laughter
explodes all around you.

Busting guts
and breaking wallets

while the whirling dervish whirls
the drinks keep coming
and the gods fight futilely to hold back
the honest roar

of their thunder.

Spandex and Issues

When I was younger
my father was a man.

When he reached middle age
he started wearing spandex
around the house
and would eat nothing but chick pea salad
and wheat grass shakes.

He took a new girlfriend
fresh out of high school
and did his Buns of Steel
to please her.

When the cherry red sports car
appeared in the driveway
my mother took the hint
and moved on.

She took him for everything
he had
but he kept his Buns of Steel
and his closet full
of spandex.

The Woman Who Works Lingerie

tries to make A-cups
not feel cheated

and fit B-cups
for the nunnery.

C-cups represent 80% of her sales
and D-cups demand
her ire.

The woman who works lingerie
directs E-cups to specialty stores
and suggests that F-cups

order online.

Anything after that
stars in Japanese monster movies.

Levelling Tokyo
with indiscriminate fury.

Redneck Ant Farm

The redneck across the street
with his rust wagon on concrete blocks
and car parts strewn about the lawn
likes to sit and drink away the afternoons
in a green plastic lawn chair
and grease monkey wife beater

and whistle at the schoolgirls as they pass
in the street.

His twin pit bulls on chains
are driven into frenzy
with each passerby
and try to eat through the chain link fence
with rabid ferocity.

To keep himself entertained,
the redneck across the street has an ant farm
he picked-up at a garage sale
which he shakes as he finishes off each beer
and lets out a hideous belch
which acts as a starting pistol.

Telling the ants that survived the latest earthquake
that it is time to start building

again.

The Young Republicans

held meetings at the community centre
with white glazed doughnuts
and instant coffee.
The folding chairs had been donated
by the local legion
and the tables by the Knights of Columbus.
Every week it was the same.
Limiting big government
anti-abortion
the right to bear arms
anti-immigration.
There was a basic fundamentalist
family values vibe
to the whole affair.
When the speakers were done
and all the chairs put away
everyone got in their American made cars
and drove home
to meet their parents

who were just getting back
from a white hooded meeting
of their own.

Looking for Lovers?

There is a guy
who stands at the corner of my street
each morning,

picking his nose
for the better part of an hour.

I stand by the window
and watch him
in morbid fascination

while he greets his neighbours
as they head off to work.

Dressed in nothing
but his housecoat and slippers,
the guy
who stands at the corner of my street
each morning

picking his nose
for the better part of an hour

has a cup of coffee,
but he does not drink it.

He just splashes it out
over the side of the curb
in small increments
until the hour is up
and he is done picking
his nose.

He then heads back into the house.
Lowering the automatic garage door
behind him
before peering out of his own

front window
moments later.

We usually ignore the intrusive presence
of one another
but sometimes exchange the odd wave
or awkward nod

as we both watch the guy
up in the tree
five houses down
who feeds the birds sunflower seeds
as he uses his binoculars
to peer through the bedroom window
of his ex-wife.

Looking
for lovers,

I'd imagine.

The Bottom Line

When the average age
of a town
is 56
the ambulance in the driveway
means a new home
will soon be up for sale.

And anticipation will mount
as concerned neighbours
gather in the street

to inquire as to whether the beautiful old lady
a few doors down,
god rest her soul,

had two bedrooms
or three.

Bonnie and Clyde

My old lady says we make a pretty good Bonnie and Clyde
as we sit around drinking cheap wine
and smoking cheaper cigars
while we look through a shoe box of old pictures
at 3:20 in the morning
and wait to call in sick
in a few hours.

She always calls first
and blames her truancy on girl problems
whenever she gets a male supervisor
on the phone.
An alternating rotation of migraines
sickness of imaginary children
and deaths in the family
seem to appease the female supervisors.

When it's my turn
my old lady does everything she can
to stop me from blaming my absence on mid-East terrorists
a clingy blowup doll
or the treachery of duplicitous chalk boards.
Once, I just told them I was too drunk to come in
and I wasn't finished screwing my old lady anyways
and they told me not to bother to come in,
but most the time I blame food poisoning
or a persistent flu.
I also use a death in the family from time to time
because I like to imagine various family members dead
and something about full creative freedom
when choosing who dies
and how
is always appealing.

When we're done making our sick calls
my old lady turns up the Chopin
and I crack a fresh bottle of wine

and we sit there together
as the sun comes up,
sorting through a shoe box full of getaway vehicles.

Death of a Motivational Speaker

A crowd gathers 'round to watch
a monkey in a sweater vest
and duty free sombrero
ride a dog around the block

as thick and greenish-yellow chunks
slide down the back of my throat
and I think of all the playground
children

in line
to use the slide.

In the end,
large smiles do not save you
from small tragedies.

Forced ones
save you from nothing
at all.

Shoplifter

Prying the choke
with a screwdriver,
I hopped in the Lincoln
and drove to the *Eastman Pharmacy*
two blocks away.

The man behind the cash
eyeballed me the whole way
as I headed to the back of the store
to renew some prescriptions.
The kid behind the pharmacist's counter
said it would be a ten minute wait
and I flipped through some
glossy bulimics
to kill the time.

After I bored of the magazines
I went aisle to aisle.
I watched an old lady
load up her purse
proud as she pleased
with anything she could find.
The man behind the cash
seemed to look right at her
and he didn't see a thing.

When they called my name
I paid for my prescription
and as the pharmacist was explaining
the proper method of application
and daily doses,
some kid was busted
for stealing a chocolate bar.

The old lady walked right past the commotion
with such an impressive haul
that much of it wouldn't fit in her purse.

She just carried it out of the store
while the man behind the cash
flashed a salutary smile.

I caught up with the old lady
on the way out
and startled her as I shook my car keys
and asked her if she needed someone
to drive the getaway car.

She hit me with her purse
full of five finger discounts
and
set off for afternoon bridge.

A cruiser pulled up
in front of the pharmacy
and the kid
with the chocolate bar
was lead away.

The Fall

Headlights crawl silently
out of the October fog
like something out from
under a rock
as the acid rains pound down
on dilapidated sheds
of warfarin
where the torsos of felled trees are stored.
Piled high
like parked cannon balls
in a soggy graveyard
where
everything forgot to die completely.

Half the town is deformed
on disability
another third is in detox.
The rest of us
watch the mouldy sidings of incessant fall rains
weep through the bloated walls
and wait to be admitted for

failure to cope.

As the fogs roll closer
and the light
disappears.

Heavy Wet Pulse of the Inner Harbour at Night

I've always enjoyed sitting down by the docks
in the inner harbour
at night
watching the love lights of the city
reflect off the water
as the stench of rotted kelp
and garbage
wafts over the muggers and conmen
who feed on stray lovers
with locked arms.

Wallets
and promises are exchanged
in haste
as the tides roll in
and barrels of sewage slam up
against the docks.

I've always enjoyed sitting down by the docks
in the inner harbour
at night
as mangy strays hiss at one another
in passing
and the horns of distant tug boats
let their heavy wet pulse wail
in the dark distance.

Rivers

The best thing about the city
is that all the great rivers of the world
are within walking distance.

The bums that squat
in the car park below my apartment
leave piss trails that wind
for as far as the eye can see
when you leave for work
each morning.

On any given weekday
I can step over the Thames
and watch it collide just feet away
with a fork in the Seine.
The Amazon usually gets lost under cars
and comes out on the other side
while the Nile
starts in a corner
near an empty liquor bottle
and combines with the Ganges
over a sewer grate.

The Volga
Mississippi
Rhine
Yellow
Congo
and Hudson
all seem to intersect with one another
under the treads of hurried feet
and I often find my morning self
trying to navigate the throngs of confluences
and estuaries.

Sometimes,
I look for the flagship

of some tiny Samuel de Champlain
sailing down the hot steaming St. Lawrence
but all I find are the discarded smoking cigarette filters
of bums
which sit as history's futile long houses
along the concrete shoreline.

The bustling sidewalks outside intrude
and my mind is once again salaried
as the sleeping bag in the corner
stirs
and vomits

and all the rivers of the world
begin to set

and dry.

Heaven is a Toothbrush with Most of the Bristles Missing

Please,
no more parodies,
there is nothing left to
assassinate.

We are all gods
of the
same
shared

ruins.

A Word of Advice

Money comes with other things
but it should never be the sole objective.
The same goes for success.
They are just window dressings… and never
the window.

Remember this, my friend.
Remember this like you remember to turn
out the light.

Bon Appetit

If you don't like the taste of it
pretend you are at some high end seafood joint
that is SO overpriced that you can't afford to dislike it,
so you eat the fish that is off, the dirty clams…
That's the only way you get through it.
The horror story of human intimacy.

That's good, he said,
can I use that?

I told him her could.
And to think of the winking waiter tableside
with his trousers down
expecting an obscenely large tip
as the alternative.

He said he felt better already.
That I should write an advice column
like that bitch Ann Landers
but for men.

I didn't know why he felt better
by went along with his toast
anyways.

And our bottles clanked
when they came together
in ways people should
not.

Brownnoser

He woke up
with a sashimi knife
at his throat
and a babbling wife
and immediately regretted
that secretary in the city
who wasn't that good
anyways

the way he'd got a pager like some dry-spit pimp
all the long hours
he'd pretended to
work

how
he kept her panties
in the glove compartment
so he could smell them
whenever he
wanted

the long brown stain
down the middle
that smelled like ass

and little
else.

Chivalry is Dead as a Dried Bunk Sock Under the Bed

A scream of rape
comes from behind the dumpster
down the alley
and I walk on
knowing the hustle
well.

The white knight to the rescue
easy mark
cleaned out
with a lead pipe
over the back of
the head.

Many past friends
have fallen for
it.

A timeless tradition
for some.

And walking on to the bar
I feel good.

Some bills for drink stuffed in my sock
and a pocket full of change
for the jukebox.

Chivalry
is dead as a dried bunk sock
under the bed.

George Jones
is not.

Dreams of Marilyn

What suns
in the shallows.

The flavour
of the week.

Another Midwest brunette
turned blonde and literate
and hopeful.

Taking the bus west.
To Hollywoodland.

Dreaming of Marilyn
in Brentwood
before the Kennedys
did her
in.

Fair Trade

Balled up in bed
in a dark cocoon of ice
three fans going in the dead of January
heavy curtains to keep the world out
but it eats at you, slow and methodical
like a pile of maggots

and
people are not trading cards
but they can be

the wretched abacus hand
crunching the numbers:

Lou Reed
for a thousand new Indian peasants
to sit in the mud

lets see you call this
a fair trade…

Dylan
for an Armenian cobbler
with a limp.

For Every Dick There is a Richard

So you want a hit
radio-friendly

breaking
into the top 40
for two and half minutes
of effort

or
less.

Something
they will play on
New Year's
Eve

while
confetti falls
like governments

and a million people
break wind

and the ghost of Dick Clark
slurs his way through another
Rockin' New
Year.

Happy Face

Last week
a ten year old girl
walked up to a shopkeeper
in a market
in rural Nigeria
smiled
held out her hand
then exploded
herself.

And all the kings horses
and all the kings
men…

Perhaps
I am a fool
but I will never understand
this world.

His Luck

was not bad
because he worked
at the glass
factory

and broke
all those mirrors

like his highschool sweetheart
once said,

his luck was bad
because all our luck
is bad

in this time
and every other

and nothing
this side of death row
can change
that.

I'm Here to Tell You…

Machismo culture,
it's neither here nor there,
iron pumping spray tans
big game Hemingway staring down the barrel
at distance
all that boozing frat house imbecility—
I'm here to tell you that the Mexican
women are hard
and good people too;
I've worked the binderies with them,
the many factories,
they work hard and fast and have a quiet
gallantry about them,
the men complain incessantly about jobs they will never leave
about wives they will never leave
to anyone who will listen,
but the women, these Chicano fillies—
the young ones so brown and proud and wiry
the older ones, the matrons,
tortilla fat, calling me college boy
along the line,
they were steady and assured
rooted like thousand year old oaks…
I could never call them wise because they were not
but perhaps they were something
better.

Better than me, better than you.
Strong as any bull in the arena.

Keeping the Minutes

Let's get a drink,
I said.

You already have one.

Well, you can never have enough drinks.

That's what Dylan Thomas thought.

Oh, you're an oracle I see,
Mr. Delphi.

Weren't the oracles always female?

It's never too late for a sex change.

Now you're playing with me.

It seems you have made me, Mr. Delphi,
I'm a sketchbook on a fishhook
the next generation opening up
their pussies for business.

Can we get back to the interview?
I have many questions.

It smells so good.
It smells so good in here.
Not like death.
Death doesn't smell good.

I guess not.

If you knew death you would not have to guess.

Do you know death?

Now I am not blaming you for shoulder dandruff
but someone will.

Why is that?

*Reciprocity in all things, be it
rusty paint thinner handshakes
or the tin shanty armpit farts
of the east African
rhinoceros.*

Do you think you are insane?

*Insane is a relative term,
insane compared to what?
Insane compared to Ted Bundy
or a garden salad?*

*

The man gave me a look
then began scrawling something in his notepad.
About my assumed insanity, no doubt.
And who could blame him, he had his angle
and an article to write.
Not out of some responsibility to the reader,
but rather to make rent, pay the bills;
heat and hydro,
all
that…

Liquid Buddha of the Faded Inkblot Sun

There are no tough dead men.
Liquid Buddha of the faded inkblot sun.
Choking bird death on the rice tossed smiles of dragging
tin can weddings.

And you see the charred years
of burnt oven mitts.
The inch between thumb and forefinger
where the painted streetwalker works.
Where clocks are would tight
as the inside of green tennis
balls.

And this is a reminder, I guess,
that even the toothpaste dries up.
The exoskeleton and the rain puddle.

Mass graves, just another gathering.
Like quills on the back of a porcupine
and the modern music
festival.

Time destroys everything and
everyone without prejudice
or exception. Say what you will
about time, but it's fair.

I like time even though it is an invention.
I am an invention too.
Of egg and sperm and nothing
on tv.
The drunken three pumper.
As if Edison downed a bottle of spiced rum
and got on top of his
wife.

That's discovery.
The scientific method, baby!

Applicable results like no one's business.
The cost of diapers and pablum
etc...

Baby seats in the trenches.
Granite countertops
that smell like
ass.
I know what I am.
I know I am lacking in
some strange
way.

An idiot, fumbling past the grotto,
walking through one pile of dog shit
after another...never learning.

Pulling the hair of little sisters
that are not sisters at all
but just your beard hairs
growing old and white
and scraggly
in the mirror

in front of
you.

MAD

is more
than a magazine.

PTSD
and the many
flash backs.

Be forced to kill
your only child
by lethal injection
and you will
understand.

They put me on meds
because I cannot
and never
will.

Many stints
in the nuthouse
like talking about the end
of the world

will stop
it.

Murphy Bed

The Murphy bed
fell out of the wall
like a mass of
termites

legs folding out
to meet
floor

and I noticed
he was not drinking
like I was
drinking

the cigarette burns
in the rug

the way he kept working closer
to the drawer which held all the knives,
suspecting what I already knew,
his eyes red
and bulging bone saw wild
as he spoke

and I smiled
like a man who knows
he's about to get
it.

New Sink

The new sink goes in
which is a big thing for her
when you can't have
children.

The 86 year old electrician
who mutters to himself
removed the eye sore over the stairs
but a new sink is different.

She is the first to spit into it.
Turning out the light.
Pretending she doesn't care.

Twisting the faucets
when she thinks no one
is looking.

Like playing with her teenaged nipples
all over again.

POW

they told him
they poisoned his food
before leaving him
to eat it

or
starve

for over three
years

in a prison camp
somewhere
in the
north

without
the light of
day

telling him
his wife had moved on,
the world too.

Whipping the backs of his legs purple
with sticks of bamboo
so bags of beetroot
on grocery store shelves
would not feel so
alone.

Safe Words

You never needed television
at the Lakeshore
Motel.

All the entertainment banged up
against the paper thin
walls.

Call me this.
Put your cigarette out
on that.

More safe words
than ashtrays
in the age of

big
tobacco.

**Slavery is Too Much from Too Little
Just as it has Always Been**

She has these weird African statues
all over the house
that always look like they know
more than I do.

With strange square heads
always squatting
with hands to
chin.

And after she goes to work
I turn them all around
to face the wall
so I can piss in the cat box
in the kitchen
in peace
and not feel
so bad

about it
all.

Southern Love

Sunning on the roof of the Perdido Key condos
in the Florida panhandle.

The bikini contest across the street
hotly contested.

One after the other
in heels
prancing on stage,
I do not remember much
except Tennessee Val
and how the MC called her:
Southern Love
as she turned in a thong
said she loved a cold beer
and fishing

like I knew
she had never handled a pole
in her life
that was not attached
to a man

imagining
all sorts of scenarios
on my own
time.

Tent City

It was a birthday
and you know the one,
the mother all the other mothers hate
because she is young and hot
and attentive

and it was a tent city in there—
all us twelve year old boys
huddled together in the kitchen
watching her build our hotdogs,
putting the wiener
in the
bun

and one kid excused himself
to the bathroom
while the rest of us
stood there

and when the party was over
and it was time to go
home

our fathers came to collect us
one by one
even though we only lived a few streets away
and they had never picked us
up before.

The Magician

cut a woman
in half
with swords

and pulled rabbits
from his hat

and made himself disappear
at the end of the night
to great
applause

but the taxman
was never
fooled

not once

and prime rib
became bony
rib

and soon the beer
dried up

at a trailer park
on the outskirts of town
living with a near toothless
rodeo clown
from Carson City
simply named:
Andy.

Wood and Silence

My mother had a highschool friend
from Birchmount High
who survived on anti-psychotics.

We visited her a few times
just east of Warden
Station.

When I was young.
Sitting around that giant oak dining room
table.

In a big lonely house of wood
and silence.

Speed Demon

When the state police pulled him over
he claimed he was possessed.

Not by the devil
but rather an overwhelming commitment
to finish the
job.

In a stolen bread truck,
making all the deliveries.

Driving 110
in a 70.

They took him in
for mental health assessment
because no one
(the arresting officers
included)

want to work
that bad.

Love is a Motherfucker

I spill my beer
on his kitchen floor
on New Year's Eve

Nerve damage.

An old work injury
from years of menial
labour.

In the next room
his coke dealer lays out a few lines
on a cd case.

Running back into the kitchen
he tells me he loves this woman
my wife works with
on a sex line.

I tell him she entertains
many strange men
one after the
other.

Much unprotected sex.

That syphilis
can be common as
hiccups.

But still
he is not deterred.

This is love,
he is certain.

I give him her beeper
and he leaves
a message.

Genocide is Cruel, Your Friends Can be Even Crueler

Finger
in warm water
and you piss
your pants.

A sleepover right
of passage
old as time.

Thank god
I was an insomniac.

Still awake
after all those horror movies
where everyone is decapitated
in under two
hours.

Always laughing
at the first to fall
asleep.

The sleeping bag
that cannot stop
snoring.

Running off
to the bathroom
like a fool of human
biology.

Yet Another Fine Coming of Age Story

He turns the coffee maker on
and she chimes in:

at least you can turn that on!

He ducks his head and busies himself
as if he didn't hear.

She smacks her lips wildly
opens her legs to reveal
a great mass of tangled
hair.

I am barely 18
just up to grab some butter
for my bread.

I got some butter here, sugar,
it shouldn't go to waste.

I smile
and head back downstairs
to my basement bachelor
on Jane Street.

Knowing full well
there will be another fight
that I will hear
through the floor
boards.

Then the sound of grunting,
of slapping flesh against the linoleum
as I eat my bread
on the end of the
bed.

Children

I do not want to have children,
he says.

And she said
she didn't want children.

She was adamant.
Sure as a peanut allergy.

And here we are
three years later
with children.

Her mother is very happy.
Spoils them beyond
belief.

Well one of you was lying,
I say,
or perhaps
both.

Why else would you have
children?

I'm Confused

First
we were supposed
to kill Charlie.

Now
we are all
Charlie.

So, do I kill myself,
or what?

The Calendar on the Wall Well Hung

The written word
like a Christmas card
has an argument.

The calendar
on the wall
well hung.

Forgery
just another way
of saying:
surprise!

The food inspector
with less teeth
then a $5
flophouse

crack
whore.

The Reading

He said the reading went well
which meant that no one cared
but they applauded when they were supposed to
like they had just witnessed the Pope in Vatican City
on Easter Sunday
or something.

And no one bought the book
but everyone told him how great
he was.

The same way Everest is great
but no one wants
to climb
it.

The Rape of Baseboard Heaters in Something Revealing

I've seen it, how could you not
have seen it?

Even the National Institute for the Blind
has seen it.

There is no need for mystery here.
No Sherlock Holmes.

Kitchen mousetraps of baiting cheese.

I've seen it.
The rape of baseboard heaters
in something revealing.

My bloodshot eyeballs
black boxes
cut out of airplanes
that won't stop
crashing.

Cigarettes for sex
like flophouse
fireflies.

I don't care if you cannot
see it.

The fertility gods of Abyssinia
banging headboards of
circumstance.

All those sleepless nights
must count for
something.

Treadmills Are an Ingenious Way for Rats Who Sit in Traffic to Stay Fit

Lab rats
on the wheel
trying to get trim
for bikini
season.

Infected
with bubonic plague
to see what
happens.

Lab rats
carved up
like a Thanksgiving
turkey

that no one
eats.

An article
in the New England Journal of Medicine
that no one
reads.

Kid on a Stick

While throngs of other couples
take their dogs for walks
after dinner
each night,
there is a couple
I pass along Esten Drive North
who power walk in pink jogging suits
with their kid on a stick
in tow.

He's not allowed to let go
of the stick
and they drop orange peels
for him to pick up
so he has something to do
in silence while
his weary parents
talk over the kama sutra and
discuss what
they could have done wrong:

If the next one also turns out retarded, the father says,
we should just get a cocker spaniel.

24 hr. Kinkos

We are at the 24 hr. Kinkos
along Spadina
so he can print out his dissertation
to present to the university brass.
Something about medieval burial rites
along the Danube,
very boring.

In fact, the whole stale scene is boring.
Nothing but lipstick lesbians
and metrosexuals.

Is it always like this, I ask,
always so...sterile?

He looks over his shoulder, smiles,
says he imagines so.

Christ gave his life for this?
I'd demand a refund.
Not one brave soul photocopying his posterior
at 20 cents a copy.

20 cents a copy!
20 cents a copy!
No sense if you ask me.

*Do you realize how many drinks you could buy
with that money?*
I ask my friend.

He laughs like I'm being funny
when I'm not.

You think Burroughs did this shit, I ask,
*stood around all night in a bloody Kinkos
waiting for a paper jam?*

My friend laughs again.
I must be a very funny individual.
Like some astronaut newly returned from space
showing pictures of the earth to his friends
who would much prefer to be looking at the pages
of Penthouse.

It's important, my friend says,
the culmination of six years of study.

He tells me that once your dissertation has been reviewed,
you have to stand in front of a three person panel
and make your case.

A sort of parole hearing for the rich,
I suppose.

The Shoplifters of Singapore

The shoplifters of Singapore have a problem.
The authorities have adopted a zero tolerance policy toward petty theft.
If you are caught stealing, they chop your hands off.

I saw a thing about it on the news, all these men and women
walking around without hands, he said,
the shoplifters of Singapore.

And everyone knows why they have no hands
so there is a form of communal shaming.
They can't find work or drive a car or anything.
Worst of all, you got all these people who would like to jack off
but can't: men, women, even children…
There are now these agencies sprouting up all over the country
that offer to send someone to your house for a fee
to get you off.
You just give them your preference: man/woman etc.
and they're at your door in under an hour.

I tell him that sounds very forward thinking.
Many repeat customers, like the drug trade.

Yeah, the only thing is, you have to prove you can't do it yourself,
that you don't have hands.

What if you don't have feet?, I ask

Then you're shit out of luck.

If Only Animals Looked Half as Good as they Taste

Vegetarianism is all the fashion.
A trend like death by stoning was a trend.

But all things pass.
Think kidney stones.

Leather interiors the used
to moo.

You'd be hard pressed to find anyone
this side of sanity
who would argue that watching
a field full of grazing cows
tastes better than a bacon double
cheeseburger.

A Smart Business Decision

The mob threatened
to break both his knees

and told him they had his wife
followed everywhere

and showed him pictures
of his children
at their school

and then
he made a smart business
decision.

Deciding to take their offer
and swallow the loss
off the books.

So he could go home each night
to his wife
and hug his kids
and ask them about their day
at school

and thank the good lord
for all his good fortune

on two bent knees
that would not require

general
reconstruction.

Not Death, Just Taxes

The coroner unzipped the body bag
and the man inside was still alive.

Since the death certificate had already been filled out
and sent to the notary
they made the man sign many papers
that said he was indeed alive
and not dead.

And then the gas company
and the hydro company
and the credit card people
began calling
again.

The taxman lying in wait
like a pride of hungry
lions.

Some Men Get Less for Murder

Her husband knew she was hard to please
but the waiters did not know that.

The chef could not have divined such things
as the order came in.

And he sent out her roasted chicken soup with mixed greens
and it came back:
undercooked.

So the chef cooked it a little longer
but it came back again:
overcooked.

The wait staff seemed a little flustered
but remained courteous.
A manager was summoned to explain the shortcomings,
then waved away by a hand.

All the restaurant patrons were whispering now.

The husband was used to this.
26 years, some men get less for murder.
He ate his meal in silence.

When the roasted chicken soup with mixed greens
came back a third time
the entire kitchen staff took turns spitting
in the soup.

The chef then sneezed all over some complementary rolls
which were sent out with the meal.

This time it was acceptable and the woman ate her meal.
Complaining all the while, but she ate it.

And later that night she was violently ill.
And had something else to complain about
that was not her husband of 26 years
for once.

Mean Muggin' the Baby Jesus

There is this garden gnome along Spine Road
with squinty eyes
and its lower jaw slung
out.

Dressed in sickly green overalls
with two vomit-yellow buttons
by each shoulder.

It is the ugliest looking thing this side of spina bifida.
I do not even know where you would find such a thing.
Or who would deign to sell it.

But there it stands, day and night.
Perched atop the crumbling front stoop of a semi-detached
with a red four door in the driveway.

Across the street
from the crazy lady with her year round
nativity seen.

Mean muggin' the baby jesus
and mary
and joseph
too.

Something to Remember

This
is
not
India.

No
sacred
cows

here.

First Love

She said her first love was a guy named Jerry
who she had dated for almost seven months
back in highschool
but he knew that was not true.

All those hours in front of the mirror.
The many oils and anti-aging creams.
Who needs 47 different hairbrushes to brush their hair?

No, Jerry was not it.

You can only have one first love
and her first love had always been
her only love:
herself.

And she was not alone in this.
Not by a longshot.
There is a reason the glamour rags fly off the shelves quick as birds of prey.

And he told her his first love had been a goldfish
named Goldie
that went belly up
when he was
four.

And she laughed like he was lying
but he was not.

Then she checked her hair in the hall mirror
as it had been nearly three and a half minutes
since her last preening
and something could have been terribly
terribly wrong.

Vlad the Inhaler

He wanted to be a vampire
so he climbed into the coffin.

It was frilly and ill-fitting
and uncomfortable.
His asthma acting up, he became short of breath.
He could never sleep in there.

So he climbed back out
quit his job at the blood bank
the very next
day.

And went back to school—
with all the 40 something housewives
of unsatisfying sex—
to study to become a corrections officer
so he could lock people in a cage
and get paid for it.

Girl in the Park

The girl in the park is dressed in tight blue jeans.
The girl in the park is in love with another.
The girl in the park bends down to pick daffodils.
There is a nice view from my window.
Little traffic and many dragonflies.

And the giants of the Solomons live deep in undiscovered caves.
And that's where I live too, my cavernous mind of gnawing.
Now there is a tiny white dog on a lead
lifting its leg over the green grass.
The girl in the park sits on a swing
and clasps her hands—
motionless, with no one to push her.
I'd like to push the girl in the park but then she'd know.
Tight blue jeans and wrinkled blouse half unbuttoned.
The tiny white dog now humping the leg of its owner has the
right idea
within its limited scope of reason.
Daffodil petals picked away like eyes from the sockets of
yesterday's many forest things,
a warm and pleasant day, whole lives legally parked:
bricklayers troweling on the slab,
and my tilted love thing in the park
passing gas when she thinks no one is looking;
a thick cloud hangs over this city, this mind

as starfish
on distant beaches
play at cartwheels below
the waterline.

A Freezer Full of Bovine Ejaculate, in the Month of Taurus

She wanted to know what I had in my freezer
and I told her it was bovine ejaculate.

You mean…

Yup, I toasted the air
as if there was only one more day
of breathing.

She made that squinty-eyed face of disgust
that women who shove zucchinis up their ass
often make when they're not sodomizing themselves with half
the farmer's market,
like YOU are doing something weird.
As if you say nice things but really want to cut off all her fingers
and sauté them with butter
and asparagus.

Why would you have that?
she moved away on the couch.

Is this not the month of Taurus?
I asked.
I'm going to artificially inseminate your stuffed animals while you sleep.
Their children will be cute and cuddly, but strong.

In truth
I hadn't the faintest idea
what was in my freezer
and what was not,
but being such a ladies' man
I knew how much women love
to be surprised

and went with
that.

Between Cinder Blocks the Mad Heart Plays

Make what you will
of anything
and it will still be
anything

and not
something.

Other things
can be something
but not anything.

A slipknot is something
a bridal gown and a picture frame
and maple syrup and a long haul trucker
too…

Your precious little anything is different.
And forever yours to make with what
you will

but it will still be anything
and you will always just be something
and not anything.

Capiche?

Toaster Ovens are Hot, but this was Different

It was after last call.
The manied meathead bouncers having got their fix.
It was in some back lot off Spadina
where his girlfriend said she had to go
whipped her pants down over her knees
and let it come.

Isn't she hot? my friend asked,
hitting me on the arm.

And yes, I had to admit
she looked pretty hot.

Under the low slung super moon.
Staring straight into my drunken eyes
and smiling.

Squatting over the pavement
as a trail of something dark and wet
and intoxicating
slowly snaked its way

toward my
shoes.

Bedtime Stories of the Damned

My uncle from Guyana
warned against wearing rings
on your fingers
when I was
five.

He told me the thieves did not take the time
to ask.

They just cut off your fingers
for the ring
and threw away the fingers
later.

2 Razors

It is our anniversary.
We have had a good dinner and watched a movie.
Now I crack the wine and pour two.
She makes a toast, takes a drink
and smiles.

Just you wait and see what I've done for you,
I used two razors.

They've been clear-cutting the Amazon for years,
I say,
why not do your part?

Her face reddens.
She is embarrassed.
That is not what she meant.

Hell, once the 70s were over
all those young birdies who gave up on feminism
to settle for a house and mortgage
had to take a weed whacker
to that thing.

Now she is more embarrassed than ever.
Drinking a little faster.
I gulp mine down like a humpback whale
with a mouthful of krill.

2 razors is not that bad,
I offer.

She puts her hand over my mouth,
begs me to stop talking.

I do,
but keep making muffled noises from under her hand
so it sounds like I am trying to speak
when I am not.

oh Nietzsche!

trying to replace Christianity
like one replaces
a lug nut

wanting to re-order a world
without order

to open a school
and spread your teachings

with an attractive young woman
you thought a fitting understudy

before she introduced you
to that other gentleman
and the many wines
of Italy

and asked you to partake
in a threesome

instead of that other
silly little enterprise
you seemed so
hung up
on.

Lighter Fluid Skin Melting Away like a Cheese Fondue

Lighter fluid skin melting away like a cheese fondue.
Night sweats through the bunching sheets of forever…

And there's the issue of spontaneous bleeding walls
and manual strangulation
and bodies in dumpsters
as if the great outdoors is for everyone,
another loudmouth giving the silent treatment,
dismembered in black hefty bags
behind the motel that charges by the hour,
the head gone missing
like all those smiling milk carton
children.

The Girls from the Colonial Style Bordello

They stand out front—
maybe 4 or 5—
on wobbling animal print giraffe stilt legs
sucking back smokes
like the made up faces
of Big Tabaco.

Don't their lips ever get tired of sucking?
I think to myself,
first the john, then the cigarette
then 30 or 40 more johns
and just as many cigarette
and perhaps a whore house attendant or two
on the side;
vacuum cleaners do less.

Look at them.
Pink spandex riding halfway up the ass
arms at the sides trying to obscure the stretch marks of pregnancy
they must get tired of sucking.

For a pittance I could find out
but I'm a coward.

I could know what a few thousand men already know
like shared knowledge
but I slink away.

Heading over to the kiosk
where the old bag with the white beard
sells shrunken
heads.

Try this one, she grins,
to protect you.

I look back at the girls

then pay my
$2.

I hear a few of the girls laughing
as I shuffle away
with my tiny
heads.

A Million Laughs that No One Else Ever Seems to Hear

He said he worked the 3 to 11
packing fudge
at the Northwest Fudge Company
on Spritzer.

So you're a fudge packer,
I laughed.

The room went silent.
No one else seemed to think
this was funny.

Like the time that dude a few years back
got his girlfriend impregnated
after a broken condom
that came from the very factory
where he worked as quality
control.

The Little Arm That Could

You know you're hard up
when even the drive-thru ignores you
and there was this party
and I got very drunk and invited myself
and there was this guy who liked to play the hero
who said something he shouldn't have
and took a swing
so he ended up on the floor
with his arm twisted up
behind his back
as I told the story of the little arm
that could—

of how there once
was this arm that wanted to be a tree branch
but was only just an arm
until one day
through sheer will and circumstance and force
it snapped,

and all the trees of the forest were impressed
and all the branches of those trees snapped
in solidarity
with the little arm that could

and when I was done telling my story
our hero, now face down on the floor
with bone protruding through skin
would not stop screaming

and no one else had anything
to say

so I left the party
and stumbled a few streets over
to where the cars sat unhappy marriage parked,
puking on a manicured hedge line
that someone had obviously
taken much care
to trim.

Rocket Attack

the
rocket
made
impact

and
she
let
out

a
little

moan.

Brazilian

She opens her legs
and smells like mouldy cheese
in some distant French
cellar.

She smiles
playing the angel,
the cum dripping out of her box
and running down her naked
inseam.

The pusey oozing of sickness
and disease.

It is a foul sticky yellowish white
like quick-dry glue
that flakes
away.

See, she says
preening from side to side,
the China ladies at the cooter cutters
gave me a Brazilian.

I ogle her throbbing flushed beef curtains for a moment
nod in the affirmative
then begin unbuttoning my work shirt.

You're late, she says,
I couldn't wait.

Then the angel is back,
smiling again.

She is pleased with herself.
The same way down syndrome feels
after making it through dinner

without drooling.

But of course, she has.
A slobbering Brazilian mess of it between
her legs.

I fall back onto the edge of the bed
and begin unlacing my work boots.

Knowing somewhere
there is a large purple ribbed dildo
resting up
after putting in a long day
as well.

While the Fingernail Pullers of Iran Share Tea

He said he was going into insulin shock
which was another way of saying
his wife had left him (again)
and took the children
and he'd lost his job because of the sadness
and now he lay hung over.

On that couch wrapped in plastic
making the face of a slobbering overfriendly dog—
the quivering jowls, those eyes so wide
and watering
begging me not to leave him
as well

like he'd sniff around the puckered bunghole
of Christ himself
if it meant I'd stay another five minutes
telling him everything was going to be okay

which I really could
not.

For Your Viewing Pleasure

First the woman came in.
A gringo girl, blonde,
just like the Chicanos liked them,
sprinkled in many oils
hamming it up for the
crowd.

Then they brought in the donkey
stage right
from behind a musty brown curtain
and forced it to mount the woman
from behind
with a series of ropes
and pulleys.

And I thought of Catherine the Great.
All those animal rights crazies throwing buckets
of their menstrual blood
over glamorous fur-coat
celebs.

But this was Mexico.

Life was cheap.
The drinks too.

And the way the donkey squealed
you could tell it wanted no part
of that woman.

As if it had been a man of God
or a pencil sharpener
or a raging
homosexual

in a past
life.

Dumpster Dive

They back down the alley
like sodomy has brake lights.

A husband and wife team
in their early 40s
perhaps.

The husband jumping out of the passenger side
as soon as the car comes to a stop,
the wife behind the wheel.

I watch from the 4th floor window
of my apartment
as he pops the trunk
then lifts the lid of the green dumpster
and climbs in.

Sorting through hypodermic needles and bags of dog shit
and broken condoms
until he finds what he's looking for.

Quickly throwing a few hefty bags
in the trunk
like the mob in reverse.

Whistling twice to his wife
so she knows when he is done.

Hopping back into the car
before they drive off down the alley
with their haul.

Electrical tape around the doors
like a poor man's
racing stripes.

Sad, the Same Way Clearance Sales Are Sad

The highschool girls
troll the bars
underage
each weekend
in their mother's clothing,
thinking it makes them
look older.

While their mothers
are at home
rifling through their daughter's
wardrobes.

Two divorces in.
40 hit, like a line of latitude no woman wants.
One last chance at love.

Looking for something they can still squeeze into.
Thinking hip huggers will make them
look younger
instead of

the
other.

This is What Got the Hindenburg

First there was Aristotle
then Newton
and Einstein

the human condition
is one of rabid
curiosity

of hypothesis
and experimentation,

so I was not surprised to walk in on them—
two grown men
each raising children
and holding down jobs

giggling like schoolgirls
with each fart,

legs in the air
the lighter in place
ass cheeks spread apart
like a fire breathing
dragon.

Beluga Joe

I tell her I was in the mouth of a whale
and she says that is not very nice
to say.

That even if my ex was a little on the heavy side
I should not say such things.

For three days and nights, I survived,
just like Jonah.

I doubt she gave you a blowjob
for three days and nights,
she retorts.

Well it seemed like three days and nights,
I say,
and perception is nine tenths of the law.

I think you mean possession.

What?

Possession, she laughs.

Possession is for exorcists
and real-estate brokers from
the Levant.

Whatever, you weren't swallowed by a whale.

But I am adamant.
I was swallowed by a whale.

And like a pro
she changes the subject.

To instances of cloud-seeding in the twentieth century
and all this rain we've been
having.

Meth Lab

It is good to see the entrepreneurial spirit
alive and well, young people branching out,
diversifying, not doing what their parents did
or their parents before;
people coming and going like books
checked out of the library
banging on the door at all hours:
shaky, thin, in tatters—
up on lifted feet, peering into darkened windows,
a blue stained mattress in the front yard
nearly swallowed up by overgrown brush
there is no one to cut the lawn
the great indoors, everyone busy inside,
and when the cops come finally
they will find all those funnels
and something on the stove
that is not mother's
cooking.

Aerial Bombardment

There are laughing frisbee kids
and picnic blanket spreads
and dogs off the chain, and masochists still on it;
the dominatrix runs a tight ship
of lust and leather,
putting out cigarettes on rosy safe word buttocks,
and there's proud fathers pulling their bike path progeny behind them in red wagons
a green canopy of thousand year old oaks
and a bronze statue of a soldier
at the ready
to commemorate all those that died
in some war
or other.

And the birds overhead take turns.
Flying low in formation, in waves.
Crapping all over the soldier.
An aerial bombardment.
Dripping from the head to the shoulders
down over the plaque at the base.
Baking on dry and white and persistent in the noonday sun.
No one from the city cleans it up.
The Parks and Rec. people seem much more concerned with the rec.
Plenty of sick calls.
No one pays the soldier any mind.

Not the kids nor their parents
nor the dogs nor the fetishists
nor the oaks…

The war is lost.

Tall Order

I am in this taco joint off the esplanade
because healthy eating is someone else's life.

Seated with my order
by where they store the napkins and the condiments
and the plastic forks that never work.

Sucking at my soda fountain drink
as I check out this outrageously tall man placing his order
at the front of the line.

6'10, maybe 7 ft.
exaggerated features, some form of gigantism, perhaps.
His clothes are wrinkled and ill-fitting
three sizes insufficient for the body they now clothe,
leathery workman's hands like two giant catcher's mitts
point to the menu.
I cannot hear what he is saying, but I imagine his voice is very low.
Very very low,
as if he were a tugboat in the distance.
Then I imagine it screeching soprano high
because this is how the gods arrange such things
they need their kicks
and we do too—
laughter is everything in a world of almost nothing,
but the kid behind the cash looks scared,
he has to crane his neck way up
like watching a flock of migrating ducks

and the line is moving slow
but no one says anything

the line is now backed up out the door
while I shove three chili-cheese fries
in my mouth

and
chew.

They Took Him Away

Alien abduction is rare
most often it ends like this—
first the men from the city with their power saws
like busy beavers
then the paramedics, and a crane
with its many winches
to lift the 800lbs shut in
cut out of his house
onto a waiting flatbed
as neighbours gather in the street
poor man, they say,
then share a laugh
while the flatbed rattles off
a blue tarp for dignity,
and a few curious children
peer inside the guts of the house
to see what they

can
find.

Buskers' Week

Everything bearded.
And 12-string acoustic.

Like you stepped back into the sixties
except the city is charging a flat fee for every corner
now.

Buskers' week.
The coffeehouses filled with condo living hipsters that complain.
About the noise, the crowds,
the intrusion…

And the many buskers, of course.
With their lacking chops, and lack of hygiene.
A few of them aren't that bad;
most are, but not a few.

It is all just recycled early Dylan really.
The same chords and strumming
without innovation.

But the tourist dollar seems impressed.
The open guitar cases lined with nickels, dimes,
quarters, dollars…

The monies often handed to a small child
to walk up and throw it in.

Like a wish fountain without the wish.
Disposable income, as the economists say.

A quick nod of thanks from the busker to the parents.

A thirsty dog off the chain by their side.
Bowls of water brought out by store employees.
A few pats on the head for recompense.

For one week each summer.
The riot police stand down and let music have its day.

Nothing controversial.
Everything meant to please.

Man is a Social Network

Imagine
if you will
giving yourself a Saran wrap enema
as an act of contrition
and imagine you then videotape the act
and throw it up on the internet
to inspire others.

Your prospective new boss
doing a quick google search
and taking a
pass.

Everything
going viral.

Private messages
from some fetishist in Austria
who wants to know if you'd be interested
in shitting on him
for $500

while he
cries.

C is NOT for Cookie

You won't believe what Teri did,
she says,
*she didn't give me my weeks off
that I requested this summer
even though I put the request in two months early
and have seniority.*

Can you fight it? I ask.

*Not without much hassle.
The union will have to get involved and they're useless.
Even if I could get the time off, my co-workers that also booked the
time off will hate me.
And Teri knew exactly what she was doing,*
she complains.

This Teri sounds like a real bitch,
I say.

No, she gets the big C-word.

Not the big C, I say.

Oh yes, she laughs,
the big C all the way.

Kush Monster

He has a habit, like loading docks have habits
is the primary caregiver for his grandmother:
changing her bandages, helping her to the bathroom,
preparing meals etc.
he's over there a few times a week
her first born grandson
keeps his hair short and respectable
a good boy

takes the money right from the old bird's purse
and convinces her she must have spent it
that her Alzheimer's has made her forgetful.

You know how you get, granny,
let me put you to bed…

Then he's off to his dealer
to make the exchange.

Like a tooth fairy
for the new
century.

The Bomb is Just Something they Hold Over Your Head, like Rainbows

The end
of the world
will never happen.

There would be nothing
to torment you
then:

to make you wake up
before the sun
each morning
work a job you hate
to pay for a family
and life

you grow to hate
even worse.

Rest assured
the bomb
will never be dropped,

so you can work forever
and ever and ever…
just like your children
and their children
and their children's
children

long after you're
gone.

Ass Slinky

She is online shopping for sex toys.
Has been talking to some of her girlfriends
and now we have disposable income.
The site she is at claims to be promoting
"female sexual wellness".
I did not know that was a real thing
but they've lined up a cadre of healthcare professionals
to attest to as much.
There's a price for female sexual wellness, of course,
plus shipping and handling.

She is scrolling down the page
past many strange contraptions.

Look at that one, I laugh,
it looks like an ass slinky.

It is very large,
a mass of metal coils
that the advert says is meant
for your anus.

My god, she laughs,
what is wrong with people?

A lot,
I say.

She keeps looking.

I Wish I was Charles

The woman who comes knocking on my 2am door
seems all business.

Are you Charles?
she asks.

No.

This is room 302 right?
chewing gum like she's
bending glass
in there.

Yeah.

She looks down at a slip of paper:

Charles
room 302
a half and half
$150 up
front
under the name
Mandy?

I tell her I am not Charles
and she seems disappointed.

Like her pimp may slap her around
for the indiscretion
and maybe cut her,
like there's a kid or two
at home
that may have to go a few more weeks
without diapers.

Curled Hair That Wants to be the Number Six

It snaps—
and you'd forgive me
for thinking of lobsters
in some nice joint by the sea
dipped in butter,
or the branch of a plum tree
under the weight of unseen masters,
but standing over the sink
looking down into the grimy Sunday basin
I see a curled hair that wants to be the number six
but what you want to be and what you are
is often two different things
and the hair snaps,
my angry fingers acting of their
own volition;
the many toilet sounds behind me
as if not only my face
has been
flushed.

Rust Proofing Your Urethra

Am I fucked up?
You bet.
There are professional assholes
and many medications
and an insatiable need to keep writing things
when no one is listening.
If you have read this far I will assume you are interested
and likely just as much the degenerate
as I.

Rust proofing your urethra.
Yellow cake uranium birthdays never getting old.

Are you fucked up?
You bet.
Fighting over limited box store parking
under the late afternoon sun
as if your very life depended
on it.

Hank Williams

had
spina
bifida

eleven
number
one
hits

and
many
pills
and
bottles

and
on
New
Year's
Day
at
the
age
of
29
out
front
an
all
night
diner

someone
asked
if
he
wanted

to
eat

last
words:

I
do
not.

Carwash

The humidity climbs through the air
one hand after the other
and I walk around the side bay door.

Pencil sharpened hand grenades
and I put the empties in the trunk
and pull out two new beers.

I am unemployed.

My friend Maddox works evenings
at the carwash
long after it has closed to the public.
Detailing cars for the Chrysler dealership
across the street.

With a dirty wash rag
and a green pail of soapy water
and some wax.

The radio blasting out
the popular sounds of the day.

Neither of us says much.
We are both quiet by nature
and there is little to say.

Only a few mumbled words here and there:
ride hot high, carwash muffin…
a secret language between friends;
the odd grunt of approval
as we tip the bottle back
let the beer run down
our gullet.

Besides, the music is very loud.
Disc jockey giveaways on the hour.

Win two tickets to see so and so at the Docks
if you're the fifteenth caller.
And some kid with a lisp calls in, very excited.
The fourteenth caller.

They sure have their fun, don't they?
The hangman dragging things out.
String a man along until he's trusted shoelace pliable.

But we are alone.
No need for such things.

Privacy is not a right, but a function.
No different than your car keys.
It serves a purpose.

And the carwash is back off the street
and it is night
and no one bothers us.

It is nice.

Maddox only works a few minutes
here and there.

Never enough to work up a sweat.

Mostly
we just drink beer
and smoke weed.

There is a compartment in the back of the radio
that comes off
so the employees can store their baggies
in there.

Each shift is responsible for rolling a few joints
and storing them away

for the next.

Real egalitarian like.
Not how the rest of the world operates.
But there are a couple leeches in the carwash employ.
There are always leeches.
As long as there has been the lifeblood, there have been leeches.
Everyone knows who they are.

Maddox is not one of them.
He keeps the radio well stocked
and his trunk full of beer.

My job is to return the empties to his trunk
and bring back two new bottles
for us to suck on.

Maddox lights another joint
and we pass the hot potato.

But not like in the schoolyard.
No one in a hurry.

Taking long deep drags
then out through the nose.

Getting the essence
and the moment.

The bay door left slightly ajar
so we do not hot box the place
in case the boss were to stop by.

But he hardly ever stops by.
More often than not, it is Charles that stops by.
Charles is the resident dealer.
He is a tall wiry skin headed type
a few years older than us

who talks a lot.

I guess dealers have to be personable.
Like call girls and the service industry.

And we smoke with Charles.
He has a million stories.
A few may even be true.

And we smile and give a half listen.
Polite, but knowing.

Maddox finds a black shiny cross under the passenger seat.
No one believing in God, but each wanting it.
I pocket it quickly and neither willing to go digging into another man's pants
the others give it up.

Small victories.
Like flatulence going unnoticed.
A good buzz going.

The radio restocked, Charles leaves.
After a quick beer he is gone.
We are both quiet and big drinkers and I think that spooks him.
People should have something to say.
We do not.

Maddox is more talkative then me
but only because he thinks he has to be.
He still lives at home with his parents
and you know how parents can be.
Ask a question, expect an answer,
your first born son should speak the language;
real inquisition shit.

But I couch surf when I can,
sleep outside the rest out the time.

My deficiencies are overlooked.
The same way everyone claps for the retarded kid
who makes boo boo in the communal
drink fountain.

With Maddox pretending to work again
I lift the bay door
stow away for a few minutes.

The moon barely visible.
The back of my hand too.

I strain to see two cats fornicating
by the back fence line.

A large black one mounts and bites down
on the ear of a bony calico
that lets out an ungodly yowl.

In seconds it is over.
The tom catting Casanova turns then shuffles off,
a job well done.

His haunches are fat
and assured.

The calico sits in the grass a few moments
hisses in my general direction
then scurries off.

I wonder if Darwin got drunk
and watched felines do the nasty?

That would explain a lot.

I bet Mrs. Darwin was a belly dancer
from the English midlands
who made a mean meatloaf.

As if step ladders should be pimped out
to housing projects.

Nightclubbing the North Atlantic seal
off the endangered species list.

Girls of sweat and strobe and bass line.

A sub-woofer in the waiting mouth of God,
anybody's god who may want one.

The turrets
of low cut tank tops
smiley face
gyrating.

Long lines for the bathroom.
The drinks watered down.
The beer recycled.

The carwash out by the city limits.
Wash. Rinse. Repeat.

Maddox throws his rag down
calls me over:
That's enough, I'm done for tonight.

He empties the pail of soapy water
into a waiting drain in the middle of the bay
turns off the radio
puts the wax away
locks up.

He punches in a security code
like the world should
never know.

I load any remaining empties into the trunk

and get two new ones
for the ride home.

Then it's back across the 400 south
weaving in and out of traffic
to the Essa Road
turn off

so Maddox can turn the music down low
and place his order

pretending he is hungry
so he can chat up the Wendy's
drive-thru
girl.

Martha's Table

The lines are long each morning
out front the OATC.

Up Princess Street
in Kingston, Ontario
waiting for their methadone.

Shaking from withdrawal
and feeling like shit.

Some of them with sleeping bags
rolled halfway up their backs.

A few of the hoarders maneuvering their shopping carts full of
tin cans
into position
like parking a late model
car.

Later, it's the two block shuffle
to Martha's Table.

To shoot the shit
over a warm
meal.

The lines are long here too.
No shortage of the needy.

Chain-smoking addicts
battered women
recent parolees
the mentally ill,
sharing stories
like it's open mic night
for those that piss in jars
and sleep in
stairwells.

On the Mend

The sickness is over,
the personal sickness anyways.
I am carrying a tissue box around the house with me
at all times,
emptying like the contents
of a recycle bin.
Clear now, not the chunky yellows
and greens
of impressionism.

And my thumb is black.
Blood has collected under the nail.
After slamming my finger through the ceiling
trying to end the days of some winged
buzz thing.

And I can hear it behind the couch.
And the sound is purse-snatcher constant.

Deaf for a week
my hearing has now returned.

Walls are not as foolproof as one
would think.

The fine young gentleman next door
gives his old lady
quite the thrashing.

She pleads with him before each blood-curdling scream.

Yes, my hearing has definitely
returned.

Khmer Rouge Does Not Make You Look Pretty

Every day
her mother and her
were marked for death.

In the killing fields of Cambodia.
Standing in line.
Waiting.

But they always ran out of bullets
before you got to the front
so you stayed alive.

The men all killed first to eliminate the threat,
the women were soon rescued
and emigrated to
America.

Where they took jobs as cashiers
and house cleaners
and masseuses that offer extras
(if you're not a cop),
always marveling at those around them
that complained about their husbands
who were never there for them
emotionally.

A Little Bit Country

She said it would be fun to get away from the city.
That she had a friend who had this ranch.
She inherited it when her parents died.
It would be completely secluded and private.

I told her no one gets away from anything,
that travel agents are the front line
of every hustle.

But there we were a few weeks later
watching chickens peck their way
into the afterlife.

Isn't it great to get away from it all?
she said.

*The Manson family got away from it all
and how'd that turn out?*

She blows over her coffee
takes a tiny sip
and winces.

On a ranch just like this…

She is no longer listening to me.
Tying her hair back in a grey scrunchie,
she exhales with a kind serenity that makes her appear
ten years younger.

Not a petrol station within seventy-five miles
in any direction
as the sun grows long in the face

and somewhere
a hungry coyote paws at a poisonous snake
though we should all know
better.

New Canadian

The elderly Asian man behind the counter
does not speak a lick of English.

We have a problem.

It is grade eleven math
all over again.

I wish to purchase X amount of goods
in Y amount of time
but the new Canadian behind the cash
keeps reaching for a can
of mace.

I am my own misunderstanding,
I don't need help.

He points to the camera over the cash and I wave.
It seems he is not being robbed again.

And then we get on well.
Exchanging a half-friendly nod
before I walk out to parking
and realize I've locked my keys
in the car.

Prince Albert

He said he got a prince albert
and then he told me what that was
and I took a step back
like he had the plague.

Not wanting to be a part of it.
The many Jews of circumcision.

I thought of meat cleavers, machetes,
pocket knives in the hands
of raving banana republic
dictators.

Then his wife came out
with some beers
which made things better

but not
much.

Water Board a Gerbil, and You Still Have Disagreement

Agreement
like a rare bird
is thought to be long extinct,
then sighted in some remote Asian jungle
200 years later.

Much more common
is disagreement:

with sibling, parents, friends
parking enforcement, census takers, the church, landlords,
employers,
the law of the land…

Fresh blood
in the schoolyard
like something
just happened.

Beside the teeter-totter.
Away from prying eyes.

A few drops of honesty
in a world

of
lies.

Soda Fountain Stuck

The theatre is dark.
This is where ugliness comes to hide.
A few hours reprieve from the light.
Petty elephant men and women in a deformed and lonely world.
Sitting as close to the back as possible.
Shoving salty popcorn into irritated canker sore mouths.
A cough from the audience every so often.
Shoes sticking to the soda fountain floor.
Banging elbows with arm rest strangers.
Hair and makeup doing its onscreen thing.
The exits lit up in case of fire.
A tear from the eye.
But not for the movie.
The theatre is dark.
The theatre is dark.

His Arm Was Broken

he could not be dissuaded.
It was purple because he had gotten drunk
the night before
and passed out on his painting
of a cabbage patch.
Now he had a sling on his arm,
a cut up bed sheet like the Klan
in miniature
knotted around his neck
for effect
and he called in sick to work
and asked many pretty ladies to load
his groceries into his car
but most would not because they thought
there was something wrong
with him

and they were
right.

Puppy Mill

The puppy mill owner
changed his name after the war
and took to torturing puppies
instead of humans
because that was now frowned
upon.

It is also a lot cheaper and efficient.

Puppies cost a fraction of what it costs
to cage humans.

The gas was harder to come by
but could be used much more liberally
on the breeders that had reached the age of four
and were no longer useful.

The bitches were bred each time they were in heat
to maximize profits.

His wife did all the grooming
but she had died some years earlier
so grooming stopped.

The puppy mill owner
fed her to the puppies.

It was cheaper than buying
all that food.

For their part,
the puppies seemed much excited
by the exotic fare.

Some keeping the femurs,
arm bones etc.
as chew toys.

The only playthings many of them
would ever know.

A Speaker from the School of Divinities

Another end of the worlder,
not the damn devil again…

He was calm as he described the coming judgement.
The lake of fire as if waterskiing were prohibited.
His cadence was soothing idiot eloquent assured
and no one listened.

The music of the day came through wiry
ear wax headphones.

Others studying for law school like honesty
must be forgotten.

A few running their fingers through the primped curling iron tangles
of new love.

Some just lay in the grass by themselves
letting the bug swarms collect
above them.

Looking at their waving hand
the same way others might look
at a Degas.

Some Woody Guthrie enthusiast
always fumbling at the guitar.

And when the speaker from the school of divinities had finished,
he closed his book
turned casually away
and walked back into the Theology
building.

And no one noticed he was gone.
The same way one less anthill escapes the eye.

Modern Art, All Over the Back of the Toilet Bowl

With shorts down around ankles
I bend over
and let it
come.

Piping hot
and easy
and red wine-soaked squid ink
black.

And no one asks me what it means.
Or what I think of Caravaggio.
Or Peter Paul Rubens' *The Garden of Love* circa 1638, oil on canvas.

Then I stand up
and wipe,
adding a few extra touches
to my creation
which could be mistaken
for clouds

or sloppy brushwork
or a commentary on
censorship

if one were so
inclined.

Forced Eviction

It arrived
like pregnancy scares arrive,
something unexpected
that you're forced
to deal
with.

Taped to the door
on fine white parchment
by half past eight in the morning
as if the landlord does not like
confrontation.

Seven months behind on the rent.
Out in 45 days by law.

In the kitchen preparing breakfast.
Cream of wheat again.
Pretending nothing is wrong.

The children
plopped in front of the television
watching Sesame Street
tell them 5 is the number
of the day

when it will take a lot more than that
to cover the rent

and those self-righteous
know-it-alls from Sesame Street
should know
that.

I Can Do Anything a MAN Can

The parrots of distant pet shops lose their nerve.
The emergency room crash cart regular
bursting at the seams like a birthday piñata
and over milk and berries
she scoffs,
drunk on Vermouth and piss
and vinegar
she proclaims:
I can do anything a MAN can.

I smile the same way a loan shark does.
Peel an orange for good measure.

Then I drop my shorts
jiggling my balls back and forth
like the big hairy dewlap
of some tame and lovable
moose.

She says nothing and storms off.
Thwarted again.

Latter Day Ain'ts

He hands me a book of Mormon
says he is thinking of converting
because the Mormons promise you your own planet
when you die.

*The Christians just offer salvation, pretty meager if you ask me.
And those Islamic fellas offer many wives
but I already had one wife and she was a total bitch.
And those damn Buddhists with all their enlightenment, who wants that?
Ignorance is bliss.*

*No, the Mormons will give me my own planet,
then I'm a Mormon, hands down.*

I tell him I think that's a popular misconception,
that they only promise you some real estate
in space, not a planet,
for your lifetime of subservience.

No planet? he says
No planet, I say.

But real estate in space is dead, he complains,
*I wouldn't be able to breathe, there's no resale value,
what's this no planet bullshit?*

At first he is angry, disbelieves me.
Then he grows quiet, uncertain.
Flipping through the pages he bows his head,
grows sullen.

I tell him I believe the last step is acceptance.
He is almost there.

I'm Not Worried

The geologists are worried
but I'm not worried.

The politicos are worried
but I'm not worried.

The stock marketers, lawyers, bomb shelter doomsdayers
all seem worried beyond belief
but I'm not worried.

THE BIG ONE IS COMING!
WE'RE LONG OVERDUE!
but I'm not worried.

GOD IS ANGRY, decry the religionists
but I'm not worried.

And look at the physicists, the toll booth operators,
the buyers of gas masks…
The environmentalists, the generals, the parkers of cars, the old,
the young, the tall short fat thin…
all so raving bat-shit worried.
Wound up wristwatch tight, throwing back anti-anxiety meds like crackerjack.
Not even the entertainers able to perform (sexually, or otherwise).

What they never tell you is that
there are no worries to be had
unless you want them.

Not here, not anywhere.

And the last thing I want are worries anyways
so I'm not worried.

But you can be worried if you want to.
Pull your hair out with all the others that worry
about going bald.

A Good Company Man

Father arrives home from work
and the house goes silent.

Hide and seek
just becomes a game
of hide.

Cracking a beer from the fridge
he walks into the bedroom
without so much as a word
grabs his belt off the back of the door
and starts with the eldest.

I guess he didn't get that raise
he was hoping for.

Missed the lunch truck
by three minutes
because he was on conference
call.

A good company man.
Staying late when the bottom line requires.
The secretaries all love him.
Never a bad word.
A great guy to work for.

The younger ones crying
with shorts around ankles
only seem to spur
him on.

Everything Must Go

The Red Tag sale promised 70% off
clearance sale
everything must go
and I went inside
found something I liked
then asked the saleslady
with the pug nose
if I could get the full 70% off
plus a two for the price of one
kind of deal
since shoes were so expensive
and I didn't have
feet.

She looked down at my feet.

Oh, they're not mine, I explained,
*I borrowed them from a
friend.*

Then she smiled
and slowly backed away.

Waving security over—
some big black gent
named Garrett
with biceps big as highway overpasses—
and he was not one for small talk
most likely on parole for something that was not a
misunderstanding,
and as we made our way to the store exit
it seemed to me
the sale of shoes meant nothing
and the only thing that had to go
was me.

Like Your Very Own Pretty Little Hiroshima

So many readers of Sylvia Plath
starting out with easy bake ovens
as if the historians are right
and there should be a strong working chronology.

Such notions confuse me.
Carnivorous plants and vegetarian people.

Running a bath for the king of France,
for all my postpartum ladies of ripped stocking
and desperate smile…

But this is philanthropy in the new century:
rubbing dandelions under chipped fingernails
then clipping away the yellow
from cowardly hands.

Drop the payload, she begs,
like your very own pretty little Hiroshima.
Mouth open, tongue out…
just keep it out of her hair,
her sole demand.

Opposable thumbs
and opposable people.

The slamming headboards of single parent homes.
Beheadings uploaded to the internet.

The prison tortilla factory open 24hrs.
A little taste of Mexico.

You'll know that things are different
when bikers start going to poetry readings.

Windows Are Transparent, Governments Are Not

The paper shredder's truck
pulls out of city hall.

The two guys in the front seat
look exhausted.

Army Brat

He was an army brat growing up
and blames his many moves
on his transient childhood.

You don't know what it's like, he self-help radio whines,
to never have any friends,
to always have to start over
again.

I never had any friends either,
but I didn't have to move a stick
for that.

Rejection can happen in less than an inch
of an inch of an inch…

No need to travel.

But this one blames the army
his combat ready parents
a base commander named Hector or Harry
or something like that
at AFB Ramstein, Germany
for his present predicament.

Eight moves
in the past year.

Many more
before that.

Maybe the landlords didn't like you selling grass
to grade school children
out of the apartment
in lunch sandwich baggies?
I suggest.

*Maybe it's the way you forget to put the emergency brake on
and slide back into the road
after a night of drunken doughnuts
on the front law?*

But no,
he's sure it's the army brat thing
and he's sticking with that.

Delish

The waiter at the seafood bar
stands over the buffet
with his hand down his pants
scratching his ass nonchalantly
when he thinks no one is looking.

Then he uses his hands to restock the steamed mussels
pile the scallops into a pyramid
massage the raw oysters.

Turning back towards the kitchen he notices
me watching him
winks the wink of kings
grinning ear to
ear.

Knowing I know what he knows
just adds to his pleasure.

Ah, you got to try these scallops,
says my lady friend
with one dangling from her fork,
they're delish!

Yeah, try the scallops motherfucker,
the grinning face from the kitchen
says.

I smile
and politely
decline.

Getting Cheeky

She was hit by a drunk driver
many moons ago
and the doctors took the fat
from her ass
to reconstruct her face.

They did a bang up job.
She's a real looker now.
Goes out to the bars each weekend
with her girlfriends.
All those guys buying her drinks,
never knowing.

But each time she complains about
a new beau she has brought home
I brace myself.

She calls him a real ass
which makes me think of her face
and I cannot stop
laughing.

And if that makes me a bad person,
so be it.

But I mean, come on girl,
an ass?

Really?

Tchaikovsky was a Fruit, and so Are Pineapples

His fingers spewed of ash
as if cremation had come early,
a grey nervousness over blood-drained faces
the master of ceremonies with his mic turned off
impish armrests laying felt landmines for the brain
in fact, distant bone-shivered atolls, calico reprimands, the boasting
squid rings of matrimony, finally;
all manner of things wheeling lint-roller sped for the exits—
and after the fingers, it was the *arms legs torso shoulder head*
until there was nothing left
to write home about
so everyone could save on postage,
which was
nice.

The Seven Year Old Psychic

Drawing on the walls
in black permanent marker
is seldom a good idea

especially
when you are seven
years old

and the walls
belong to your father

and when he got home from work
(stumbling dog-whipped
tired)

the boy flinched
as if his father was going
to hit him.

Then he did.

Ode to GG Allin, I Guess

I'd like to cover myself in feces
because my father threatened to bury the entire family
in the attic
and started digging holes,
and walk the streets of New York
like some Poocasso
from the museum of modern
art

and to say what I feel
and feel what I say
(that's what it's about
right?)

and defecate
on my many fans
but I have no fans
to speak of.

Not even a few hundred
at some last chance dive in Manhattan
to be fooled into the dollar store trappings
of spinning hamster wheel
genius.

Living from a single paper bag, I get it.
The man on the go.
I understand the apparatus.
Just one question:

why commit suicide on Halloween
with so many pumpkins
about?

Everyone stealing the press
on the six o'clock news
while your death
falls like a bloody tampon

by the
wayside.

Food Court

Disagreements break out
just as prisoners break
out—
the red plastic trays of the food court
now weapons
in the hands of adolescents.

I guess it is better than guns and knives.
The missus off trying on shirts.

A heavy set black girl
from Manchu Wok
throws off her hairnet
jumps the counter
and joins in the
fracas.

Much screaming and many punches.
And the red plastic food trays,
of course.

It is all very exciting.
Everyone taking sides.

As I eat my New York fries
with white cheese curds
and extra gravy

from a
cup.

When the missus returns some twenty minutes later
they are still cleaning up.

Jesus, what happened here?
she asks.

Nothing much, I answer,
find anything that fit?

Boots on the Ground

City hall
spent five million dollars of taxpayers' money
to build a wall
for a planned mall construction
that fell through.

Now the locals get to look at a wall
in the middle of nowhere
that they paid for
each time city council votes
to raise taxes
again.

But that's still better than the ten million spent
to build a blue handicap ramp outside the old mall
that collapsed,
then the extra two million to remove it
when it wasn't being used.

But this next project is the big one,
the municipal politicos promise.

People around town are excited
because people are idiots.

Evolution my ass.
Darwin was wrong as hell.

But this is the one to put us on the map, they boast,
construction has already started.

There are "boots on the ground"
they are so fond of saying
and if you look closely
they are not lying.

There is a single pair of worker's boots

laid out in the middle of a gravel pit.

These small town lawyers
really cover all their
bases.

Volunteer Firefighters

They take turns.

Three boys
on a neighbouring lawn.

One,
the firefighter,
holding a green garden hose
and spraying his spinning companion
who pretends to be the
fire.

A third boy a few years younger,
a little brother, no doubt,
lays out on the lawn
pretending to be killed by
the fire.

When it is time to switch up
the fire grabs the hose
and becomes the firefighter
while the firefighter starts spinning
fast as he can
like a fire out of control.

The youngest one sits up,
complaining once again
about having to be the dead guy
burnt to a crisp.

Before storming off—
like the walking dead—
because he never gets to be
the fire

or the one who puts
it out.

Isaac Newton Proved Right Yet Again

The negotiator
tried to talk the jumper down
from the 37th floor of the national
credit union
but after a few hours of little progress
he no longer cared.

His heart was no longer in it.
He couldn't say why.
Usually he tried very hard.

He just figured it a question of personalities.
There are people you get on with
and then there are the others.

If he met this man under ordinary circumstances
they would likely fight over a parking spot
or the son of a bitch would butt into line
or hit on his wife in front of him
or borrow his hedge clippers
and never give them
back.

But being the professional he was
he made a show of it.
Made many concessions
brought the family in for personal effect,
but truth be told
he couldn't care less if this one
painted the pavement.

He almost hoped he did.

Another three cheese pizza
as they say
in the business.

Day Labourer

The morning work truck is full.

Both sides
of the cab.

With many sleepy pockmarked men.

I am the only one
who speaks English.

God's throwaways
as if the toilets were full
and we needed a new way.

The plunger of the workday world
pushing everyone down.

Sitting on milk cartons
passing cigarettes
under the sun.

In steel toes
and lumberjack,
our lunch buckets under
the arm.

Sharing a laugh
in spite of circumstance.

Enjoying the wind through the hair
like the poor have lovers
too.

A large confederate flag
strung up in the truck cab window
as if the boss man

may have a preference

when push comes
to shove.

The Drunken Church Sign Alteration

Some men alter pants
and others alter their testimony
in a court of law
and the United Church sign
across from the White Towers motel
had so many letters
and we'd had so many drinks
that soon
there was a convergence
of circumstance.

An unholy trinity.

One for lookout
one to separate the vowels
from consonants
and pass the letters
and another, me,
(the ever cunning linguist)
to say something unfavourable about God
to welcome the Sunday collection plate crowd
or just something
one-thirty in the morning
I just ate a gas bar cold cut sandwich
and considered it fine dining
legible.

We must have worked away
for a good twenty minutes or more on this one.
It was slow going.
The lookout trying to find singing crickets
in the grass
as he relieved
himself.

It was then that I looked up,
out of the side of my eyes.

A police cruiser at the lights
sitting mounted candlestick silent
watching us.

He pulled up on the green
(with that quick mini-siren that they do
when they know they got you
by the balls)
and got out with a flashlight
and my girl, god bless her,
went right into victimhood mode
gave him some sorry thread about
dropping her cigarette
and all of us looking
for it.

Apparently the paperwork would have been too much.
He suggested we head home now.

Just then our gay lookout—
like a Pride parade in a hurry—
began running away over the
Anne Street
bridge.

Do you know him?
the officer said
shining his flashlight
on the frayed jean short ass
hurdler high kicking it
halfway to
nowhere.

Unfortunately
we did.

Meals on Wheels

There is a sudden bump in the road
and a shared look of astonishment
as we head back home up the 108
after a day of shopping
in the city.

The heavy repetitive thud of the left front tire.
A thick red smear across the pavement
in the rear view.

Pulling into the driveway we get out.
Lean in close for a better look, but not that close.
It is hard to tell what it is
(or once was)
like trying to follow a comet as seen from the hairy puckered
bunghole
of a chimpanzee.

But there is pink innards
some patches of fur
meals on wheels,
to be
sure.

Something for the buzzards and the maggots
and the madmen who piss
in juice jars

to pick
over.

Why a New York Times Bestseller Will Never Be Anyone That Matters

To
find
fault
with
the
written
word

is
fair
game

but
to
find
fault
with
the
person

in
spite
of
the
written
word

is
just

prejudice.

Urine Pucks

We are all urine pucks, pissing on each other's lives,
scuttling the dreams of others, strangling every vague hope
into dark submission
and the few that rise up, they're the preferred: the chosen few
from all the best families and all the best schools
with all the best money, of course,
the best money being most or all the money
that the ugly masses do not have,
but even the rich piss on each other—
gossiping, disinheriting, shaming...
But who gives a damn about the rich you might ask?
The poor, that's who— the poor give a damn alright;
there would be less alcoholism if everyone had a yacht
and three butter blondes on their arm,
more cocaine perhaps, but less of the bottle
but we seem to take some perverse pleasure in meeting new people,
unzipping, and pissing all over them;
barring all hope, squandering any gains
suffocating the dream;
and no one or nothing is immune:
we piss on the planet, into the water table,
all over the plants and animals too—
URINE PUCKS, good sir, that is what we are,
no more, no less...

The gentleman shifted in his chair
then looked up from my resume:
I don't think you are right for the position,
he said,
but thanks for coming down.

I mean, I'm a hard worker, I said,
very loyal.

The position has already been filled,
he said
extending his hand like a man
who never ever wants to see
or hear from you
again.

Drive-by

Our car creeps up to a stop
beside a late model Sedan
with four young black males
inside.

I roll down the window
make a gun out my fingers
and open
fire.

They seems surprised.

Like they don't know what to do
when it's the other way
around.

Then my old lady slaps me on the chest
and I roll the window back up.

Reloading the clip
of my imaginary gun
as we drive
on.

Kiss the Cook

We sit out back among the summer mosquitoes.

Arguing the historical implications of blackheads
according to the Julian calendar.

In green fold out lawn chairs
from the seventies
with mesh backs that have
some give.

From the St. Vincent de Paul.
The sisters of mercy.
A real deal, I'm told.

Along with the tackle boxes
become window
planters.

Our host with a *Kiss the Cook* apron on.
A gift from his many children.

Searing meat on the grill
like the slaughterhouse
putting its best foot
forward.

Standing over the barbecue
smoking out the neighbours.

Then sitting down again,
re-entering the arena.

Drinking imported beer.
An imported wife to boot.

And some dog draped over his feet
like drooling slippers that bark
every so often.

Pilot Project

They started putting poetry billboards on public transit
as a way to provide some culture
and stem a rash of recent shootings.

The people no longer want to kill each other.
The poetry is there now.

Everyone now want to kill themselves
and perhaps the poet in question
for subjecting them to such
rubbish.

But they no longer kill each other.
Which is good.

Zero Sum

Lemons on the lot
all things finagled down to nothing:
the water supply, the troop supply, the job site green outhouses
of tipping;
soon we will be breathing in imported air
and paying through the nose for it
quite literally,
the many storefront awnings
just large umbrellas
of convenience
one never has
to hold.

Death Never Happens on a Waterbed

Remarkable, she said,
just remarkable…
and since it was just
remarkable
and nothing else besides,
it was easy to understand;
against all odds there
was a thin streaming
ease.

As if the gods, this world,
had faltered,
giving mercy its day
in the
sun.

Fear Keeps Many People in Work

The rains have stopped now.
I guess Noah was wrong as hell.
Noah, being those backed up sewer
avoid free flowing river alarmists
from the weather channel.

Offering the most dire of forecasts.
Often pregnant and showing,
so you know they make
mistakes.

Predicting some cyclone
or board up your lives typhoon
or some category 5 humdinger
straight out of the Caribbean

each time something simple as a shoelace
or a hymen

breaks.

sometimes

the
only
thing
you
can
do

is
leave
the
toilet
seat
up

and
wait
for

better
days.

Running the Mouth, and Not the Generator

He said he was a badass
from the mean streets of somewhere
or other
not to be messed with,
but the arrest record
was not there.

I had a friend who pulled some strings
and a Bulk Barn shoplifting gig at 21
does not make you Attila the Hun
in my books.

He said he had been in the war
and seen things.

That he was a third degree black belt.
Had been involved in the underground for many years.
Responsible for a spate of unsolved bombings
in Europe.

But this yahoo was soft.
Pinched less than goose flesh,
he spoke of his many years
on the run.

Next time he was over
we got him good and drunk on discount Cognac
until he cried in some woman's arms
in a purple blow up chair
beside a candle that kept going out.

As we fed him more and more Cognac
to keep the lying son of a bitch
talking.

And we laughed like nobody's business.
The gut beginning to hurt a little.

As the woman he was with
tried to get him to leave
and/or stop talking
but he wouldn't.

Punching my Ticket to Sainthood

Of late
I've had this recurring dream
where I am carrying one of those yellow diamond
shaped construction signs
that read: SLOW
cheering crowds lining the road
as I walk by
leading a long line of all the autistics,
the down syndromes, the low functioning
out of town

just like St. Patrick
did the snakes.

Another Position

John Nash
heard voices
like the answering machine
hears voices

rode his bicycle in figure eights
obsessively

and when the University of Chicago
offered him a prestigious post
in their Mathematics Department
he said thanks
but no
thanks

informing them
that he had already accepted
another position

as the Emperor of
Antarctica.

Tea Kettle Madness

You flip the page of the book
and it is just as you expected
(more or
less)
no surprises
not even a comma
out of place.

Why not a leper
who climbs out of a wood chipper
in the heart of lower Manhattan
jigsaw puzzle reformed?

A restaurateur who feeds his many followers
nothing but solar flares
and grits?

Pages 56 through 72 never written
so you can wonder what might have been
on your own time?

A whistling tea kettle madness
to it all?

I like the Dadaists
in spite of some of their
politics.

The lazy axle grease thighs
of failed abortions.

Character development
sour milk carton
missing.

A peace
to end all peace
as we know
it.

Finger Fuck a Hand Grenade, Things Get Messy

Bag your groceries in the scrotal sack
furry crow blast teeth a grinnin'

finger fuck a hand grenade
things get messy

folded newspaper under arm
like hot from the presses deodorant

the shiny magpie price of
never knowing.

A Coney Island of the Dogs

At Coney Island Dogs
in Detroit,
we are the only white faces
in there
and you begin to question
the wisdom of such
a venture.

At first
it seems you are not
welcome,
but the food is good
enough
and the beer strong
and the glares soon fall away
to other realities.

On the way back to the hotel
we retain a steady pace.

She keeps looking over her shoulder
every three or four steps
for an armed drug-addicted black man
in a balaclava

that never
comes.

The Talk

Son, do you know what sex is?

No.

It's when a man and a woman get together to make babies.

Like the other man?

What other man?

The man who comes to see mommy when you go to work.

What do they do?

I don't know.

What do you mean you don't know?

Mommy always tells me to be a good boy
and go down to the basement
and play with my toys.

Jamaican Shower Posses

Really, that's the name you chose?

Out of all the possible incarnations
of gang fear you came up with:
Jamaican Shower Posses.

Sorry, sounds like a gay men's club
fad to me,
group showers
of 20-30 men
giving each other the reach around
to sweaty strobe club music;
soaping down complete strangers
with disposable sponge glove loofahs
like the Roman bathhouse
brought to the new
world.

The Mob Puts Bodies Here but You Never See Them

Ever been to the desert?
I have.

The desert of too much to drink
again and again.

Calling in sick to work
with your best bubonic plague voice
then sliming back into
bed.

Between the sheets.
Between hangovers.

Dry mouth
like you can't stop the late afternoon scorpions
from climbing into
it.

Impeaching my Local Cable Service Provider

I have assassinated every living president.
Peeled the eyes off many potatoes and made them my own, ears of corn too.
I am a hoarder of many imaginary things.
I hide in linen closets not because the Chinese have the bomb but rather because I do not.
I wear a balaclava to the dinner table.
Say many things that offend.
Impeach my local cable service provider.
Artificially inseminate stuffed animals that "are trying".
Fashion my own homemade ninja stars and store them in my sock drawer.
I am the lone gunman, I am every gunman;
always with three names like a sinister game of tic tac toe.
I listen to the industrial metal concept albums of the vacuum cleaner front to back.
I crush feet under spiders, close the airspace in my pants.
Trowel deep into my neighbour's rose garden
like I could make Middle-earth
by sundown.

"Goodbye Everybody"

Never one to mince words,
Hart Crane threw himself off a boat
into the Gulf of Mexico
at age 32

while John Berryman
jumped off the Washington Avenue bridge
in Minneapolis
age 57,

into far colder
waters

after much warmer
reviews.

To the Left of Nowhere

I remember convincing my friends to play tackle football on the street,
to ice down the banks in winter so we would have something else
to smack each other into

swallowing down whole bottles of Vodka
five minutes into a house party,
wearing my alcohol poisoning as a badge of courage.

I was a true suicide case.
Full of self-hate, or maybe nothing
at all.

I always felt I was lacking in some way.
Like a Christmas tree with nothing under it.
A little off, to the left of nowhere.

The invincibility of youth, sure,
but there was always something else.

A core that could never be reached.
Both fire walker and volcano.
Like something never suppose to live could ever die.

Running across four lanes of traffic and back
on a dare,
sitting in front of the mirror
and punching myself in the face
on weekends
to toughen
up

or how I used to take my parent's old blue beater out
when I was sixteen
press my lead foot to the gas
laughing

pushing 100, 110, 120
before things began to shake,

flying over the train tracks
down through a blind
intersection

along Little Avenue
a few times a month

watching to see which of my friends
put on his seat belt first
so we would know
who was the
chickie

to be mocked incessantly

for wanting to live
and not to die

or caring

either
way.

Walmart Greeter

The Walmart greeter
is the happiest person
I have ever seen.

A 300lbs happy face
in a blue smock
just like the company
promo.

A hap hap happy minimum wage earner
of a thousand
delights.

Returning carts
and squeezing the cheeks of many young children
as if she is high on
something.

I have never felt this way about any job.

Just look at her,
so impossibly happy.

Like she's up for review
at the end of the month.

The cameras always watching.

Another child of the free world.
Acting accordingly, or else.

She must cry herself to sleep each night,
this beacon of service industry happiness.
This product of divorce, the collection plate,
saturated fats…

Alone

with a crinkled up picture of Kevin Costner
under her pillow.

Flipping through all the travel magazines
with a bottle of Jägermeister
and her seventeen cats,
imagining all the places
she can never afford
to go.

Bobbing for Apples, Well Into Adulthood

Follow the dead fly neon coin slot peep show.
The smiling bus station Midwest runaways
leaning over the passenger side door
along Sunset Boulevard
in skin tight hot pants
negotiating terms.

This is the market economy.
Everything for a price.

You can shave the legs
of lady liberty
for a fee.

Sodomize a tranny
with giant Rushmore balls
to hungry lion prides
on HBO
tearing lagging gazelle meat
from the bone.

Guide a head
bobbing for apples
well into adulthood
that promises to
swallow.

Some voodoo case
from Haiti or the Dominican
trying to make it
as a shooter girl.

The rest of the world
full of war and disease
and famine…

providing crew cuts
like even the barbershops
have grown
lazy.

Yellow Cake Uranium Birthdays

Ever seen the blue pulsing veins
of your schoolyard friend
whorehouse exposed
and throbbing?

Picked out
through layers of skin
with a bent paper clip
so you would like him
more?

Some men
do not understand decapitated birds
perched on chain link fences

or the forty hour week
brown bag guillotine
familiar

or dead cats
with firecrackers shoved up
their assholes

but I
do.

A Moment in the Sun

One forearm
was four times the size
of the other
and I smiled.

What the hell are you looking at?
he asked
accusingly.

You should really mix it up sometimes, buddy,
I said,
jacking it with the same hand
again and again
is not
healthy.

He looked down at his forearms—
held them out for
comparison—
then laughed.

Then the foreman
walked out from his
office—
slamming clipboard
angry—
back to work,
I'm not paying you jack offs
to stroke it
on my time.

The whole loading dock
broke out
in laughter.

Some sort of acute spasmodic
contagion.

The pay was lousy.
The work was lousy.
The moment was something else
and would be glorious
forever.

Genius is Sticking a Grapefruit Down Your Pants and Realizing that is One Less Grapefruit the Starving World Wants to Eat

Ever notice
that clouds cannot stop moving?
They must have some kind of ADD,
or ADHD for you High Def. snobs.
I cannot stop moving either.
I must be a cloud.
I scored abnormally high on the latest IQ test:
deductive reasoning.
You know who else cannot stop moving?
Sharks.
They must be me or clouds or both.
Or perhaps we're all just
sharks

that keep swimming and swimming
and swimming

in the
surf.

The Tongue Wresters of Modern France

The road tears itself up in protest
high rise windows shatter like glass eardrums
dirty drinking water down the waiting gullet of efficiency experts
and I think of many far off things—
honking tuk tuk armies, breaststroke festival lanterns aflame,
the newly sick and the oddly embarrassed,
tongue wresting, the national sport of the French;
in the backs of foggy cars, out past curfew:
man on man, man on woman,
woman on woman
and more...
the tongue wrestlers of modern France
a real variety show
dismembered bodies float by in the seine
wave bye to living
dogs walking dogs with slobbering anvil heads
fur traders on every street corner, negotiating a price,
hot coffee in dusty internet cafes
the guts
and the glory

the road puts itself back together
this water still dirty but I drink it.

That Million Dollar Idea is Only a Million Dollars Away

Everyone has a niche, you just have to find it.
The bearded lady should never shave.
Midgets are just skyscrapers that never made it,
but there is a niche there to be exploited,
a market for everything.

You?
You seem especially stupid and repulsive,
perhaps there is money in that.

I hear the goat boy did pretty good.
And that kid from northern India who is slowly turning
into a tree.

Me, what's my carved out niche you ask?
I plan to corner the semi-retarded market:

Drink myself into selective mutism night after night.
Give mouldy shower curtains sexually suggestive backrubs.

Roll my balled up socks into neighbourhood garden gnomes
in someone else's shoes
and call it
bowling.

French River Trading Post

We are on our way out of the north.
Heading towards the city.
We stop at the French River Trading Post
so she can use the facilities.
I head inside past the flags and buttons
and postcards.
Much patriotic kitsch on spinning impulse buy racks
by the door.
Running my fingers through a table
of white rabbit pelts
I realize it is floor to ceiling animal.
The jackets are made from the hides of animals,
the hats and pants too.
Like the slaughterhouse does its thing
and the supermarket gets the innards
and the trading post gets the rest.
It is all very efficient.
Nothing gone to waste.
Even the feet attached to silver key chains for luck.
The unmentionables smoked
and sold as jerky.

Can I help you?, the lingering saleslady asks.
No one can but I do not tell her that.

Just looking, I say.
She turns and walks off
like a disappointed
hangman.

And the great indoors leave a lot to be desired.
I admire animals of all shapes and sizes
far too much to stay in this place
any longer.

I go outside for some fresh air.
There is none.

Something with a large diesel engine
sits spewing out its guts
by the side of the road.

Parked Airstreams compete for real-estate.
Filled with many screaming children
just happy to be out of the womb
and semi-literate.

To be fed and clothed
and named.

Like a place in the phonebook is all but guaranteed.

Most will make eighty with ease.
Without ever living a single day
in their entire lives.

And such feats will become accomplishments to be celebrated.
There will be a cake and everything.
The candles put out by wetted birthday fingers masquerading as
bravery.

The missus comes back from the washroom.
That was not pleasant, she says.
Most things aren't, I offer.

Then we are back on the road.
The circling buzzards above.

Past a speed trap a few miles south
along highway 69
as if not only death should be slow
and costly.

How Come Faith Healer Never Comes Up in the Want Ads?

It's always unskilled labourer,
English an asset.

But I don't want to be unskilled labour anymore.
Chump change is for chumps
or they would not call it
thus.

I want to be a faith healer.

Rub diced carrots over the waiting bare-breasted nipples
of a never ending procession of desperate 20-something women
all wanting to be fertile
in spite of what the doctors tell them.

Magic finger fucking half the Latter Day Saints back into
parenthood in under an hour.
Praise god, almighty!

Banking some serious coin.
No one ever questioning your methods
because that would be sacrilege.
Sounds pretty good.
No foreman or super breathing down your neck.
That's one sweet deal.

Just like that guy in the southwest
who goes from town to drought-stricken town
and does a 45-minute rain-dance on the hood of his El Camino
for a small fortune

or the army of literary critics
who know
and do
even less

for
theirs.

Kingston Meats

Spending my days in the bookstore
down on Princess.

All those books.
Most of them crap, but many were not.

And I sat from around noon each day
until the store closed just after sundown.

Treating the books on the shelf
as my own private collection,
then leaving in the evening with the employees
and heading north
back up Princess.

Past the Lebanese joint
that made the best drunk food
and the family run Kingston Meats
a few blocks on.

Then I'd take the darkened side streets
towards Concession.

Past the park
behind the old memorial centre
where the many skinny jeaned boys
of the lisp
stroked each other's summer sausage
in peace.

Voted Most Likely to Succeed

The meth whore
in the stairwell
used to be a real
looker.

She shows me an old yearbook photo
torn away from the
whole.

Now,
she sits up for six days straight
giving $5 gum jobs
and reeking of
urine.

Her children in the care
of the state.

Crushed potato chips
in her hair.

A sleeping bag
under the stairs
full of cigarette
burns.

She Says I'm a Difficult Man to Live With, and There May be Something to That

So what do you think of Florida,
she asks?

2000 miles
to use the bathroom,
I grumble.

I should have stayed
home.

Money Only Knows

Money only knows that I never carry a wallet.
Money only knows that my bills are folded fast as a losing hand
of poker.
That I hang to the left in the common vein,
money only knows.

Money only knows if my balled up tissues are used or not,
if the smiling bank teller returning from the washroom
washed her hands.

They say money talks as well
though I have yet to
hear it.

Money only knows
why anything exchanges hands.

If you are being followed
or doing the
following.

No use pressing the mint for anything
they do the pressing,
money only knows
money only knows…

A Tree with Bark

Balding tree
and balding man.

A common understanding.

The thick canopy of youth
long receding.

One dying,
the other just
balding.

Prematurely
like his father and his father
before.

Then the man
took his axe
and chopped down
the tree

and used it
for firewood

because understanding
only goes
so far.

Kickers Are People Too

The kicker
was not needed
for nearly the entire
game.

Drafted in the sixth round
out of Texas Tech.

A child
among men
when it came to the weight room,
kickers are people too.

Alone in team meetings.
An afterthought in the building.

And there he sat on the sideline.
On heated seats.
Drinking Gatorade with many bathroom breaks.

Brought in cold turkey
to bank a 42 yarder
off the left upright
with no time
remaining.

Ice in his veins
according to the sports writer narrative
of the day
instead of a spot in the unemployment
line.

The hero
for another week
and not the
goat.

A steady paycheck coming in
so his wife
could begin remodeling
the kitchen.

Confessional

She tells me
she has only been with
ten men
in her life
and I think of
bowling.

One blow job
for every
pin.

The lanes open late
for those that bowl a
perfect 300.

I want to come to you honest,
she says,
*one man was married
while I worked front desk
at the hotel.*

I tell her
I'm a polygamist
with a bag full of wives
that others call my golf
clubs.

She seems angry
that I'm not being sincere.

I pull down my shorts
and tell her I'm married.

Apparently
there is a history
there.

Tiny Sunsets

LOOK AT THESE! he shouted excitedly
and I looked at the palm of his hand,
how the underside of his knuckles grew flush
each time he stretched his fingers out,
like someone witnessing a miracle
who doesn't know it—
I think there's blood in there
he said,
I think you're right
I said,
and I could tell by the way he kept eyeing
the paring knife
that he wanted to find out
but was polite enough
not to try.

Haunted Walk

The haunted walk
was for drunk American tourists
up from New York state
that had money to spend
and wanted to walk the cobblestone streets
at night
and hear ghost stories
instead of return to the hotel
by 10pm
to have disappointing
sex.

For their part,
the university students that conducted the haunted walks
dressed in black
and handed out flashlights
and really played up the whole limestone attracts ghosties
aspect of it all.

Some of them were pretty good.
Really hamming it up for tips.

Occasionally there was a heckler
but they were quickly shouted down.

No one wanting to be forced to go back to the hotel
and have sex with their lovely wives
or husbands
after twenty-five plus years
of happy marriage.

Not because some drunk asshole
decided to take issue
with casper.

SURPRISE!

She gave him herpes
like they were secret santas
and now he has these odd looking sores
around his mouth
that seem to flare up out of nowhere
like angry nostrils.
I used to bother him about it
but I don't anymore.
When he speaks to women
he covers his mouth
which doesn't help at all.
Yes, women want a sense of mystery,
but not that.
When he goes on job interviews
the position is always filled
once they get a good look at him.

I have no idea what he gave her in return.
I hope it was something good.

Because hers was a real
doozy.

On a Three Day Greyhound Back Across the Country with Four Rows of Stale Cookies and a Whole New Outlook On Life

The west is not the best, trust me on this:
should be removed from the compass
altogether.

Nothing but junkies and thieves
and bars on windows.

Grey and dreary British Columbia.

I was 22 and always cold.
Didn't see the sun for months.
Accused of stealing every store I walked into.
Couldn't find work to save my life.

What a shithole.
At least Rome rose before it fell.

I'm an Ontario boy anyways.

I much prefer reaching orgasm
in Eastern Standard
Time.

*Zzzzzzzzzzzzzz*s

Father McGregor
slept through weekly confessional
because it was always
the same:

I stole from my mother's purse
I uttered an untruth
I won at Saturday bridge unfairly…

All so very boring.
Over and over again.

He was not hurting anyone,
he just wasn't listening.

A few our fathers
and hail Marys doled out at the right time
and no one was the wiser.

He figured
he loved thy neighbour
that cut his grass for him
each summer
so it evened itself
out.

Besides
sleep was not a sin
according to the good book
(regardless of
denomination)

so what the
hell?

Get Bent

Trees can grow crooked
just as people grow crooked
and there it leaned on the summer lawn
after some midnight drunk
slurring old sea shanties under cover of darkness
tripped over the curbside
and fell into the tree.

Now it grows sideways
but is probably not aware of it

the same way your back will make faces at you
for a whole lifetime
without you
ever
knowing.

Student Painters

The student painters
were a trusted part of the community.

Making a little extra money over the summer
to help cover Fall tuition.

Rifling through jewel boxes
and drawers
while the client was away.

Fanning out in teams
to take just enough not to be noticed
or openly accused.

They came with references.
Always impeccably dressed.
Consummate professionals.

And once
they got down to painting
they did a real bang up
job.

Nudist Colony

He claimed that he had been kicked out of the nudist colony
for wearing clothes
and that when security threw him out
kicking and screaming
they had half-chubbies like they really enjoy
that shit.

I asked him why he was wearing clothes
at a nudist colony
and he said it was in protest.

In protest of what? I asked.

Everyone else gets to protest these days, he shouted,
why the hell can't I?

I shrugged my shoulders
turned and walked
away.

My own SILENT protest,
so seldom the
trend.

Bitch Be Cray Cray

A man
can never drink
his wife
away.

Everyone
that has tried
has failed.

The liver seems to go
before the
union.

In both new world
and old.

And there should be little sympathy.
Remember, you agreed.
In front of gathered friends and family.
In sickness and in health,
that's what the child molester
for hire
said.

You promised to take out the garbage
until the end
of time.

That shit is binding.

Like the glue they use
on books.

You promised, and she'll remind you of that.

To fuck her as she grows big as a house,
shoving bonbons down her pie hole

to *The Young and the Restless*,
spending your money twenty times as fast
as you could ever make it
working three jobs
that keep you sleepless space program
busy

while she screws some other dude
with a bad 80s flock of seagull
do,
and that makes you somehow angry
even though you should be birthday piñata
burst open with
joy

that there is finally someone else
ready to play

the
fool.

Genius

I could do better than Napoleon,
he bellowed
after one too many.

Of course, I said,
Napoleon married a whore
and died of arsenic poisoning
sixty pounds overweight.

But the genius, he slurred
puffing out his chest
and pacing the room with his hands
behind his back.

What genius?
I said,
any man can eat badly
be cheated on,
then poisoned.

I told him Napoleon was just a janitor
without the mop.

He grew angry
and stormed out of my apartment.

I could hear him a few moments later.
Screaming at a chain link fence up the street.

Trying to convince it
of his genius.

As I fell into bed
belly down,
wondering why I always get drunk
with such pompous little
assholes.

Parking Enforcement

They were beating up the parking enforcement officer
so I guess their time had run out.

On the other side of the street
three men in black tank tops
looking like human growth hormone
had a promising future,
raining down kicks and punches
as parking enforcement
went fetal.

Then the most veiny one amongst them
(apparently the driver)
tore the yellow ticket away
from the windshield
crumpled it up into a ball
and threw it back at parking enforcement
like the opening pitch
of the World Series.

Then the three men got in the car
and drove off.

And no one else was parked illegally
for the rest of that
day.

I Taste the Tongues that Rape Me

Do not be fooled by hair colouring,
extensions like bad marriages drawn out
by the handshake as peacemaker
or the endangered species list;
east is the new west
the compass has been wrong,
all avenues head south
when you really get down
to it

and we are little different:
all bowel and taxes and genealogy
long hours of indigestion
and clockwatching
and worship of mummified cats

but there is a carelessness to my day
which eludes your calendar
zip lines to nowhere
the invention of fire
anew…

I taste the tongues that rape me
pluck turkeys prepubescent bald with mangled vise grip
love me not hands

and there's the flood—
more idea than water
(almost always after
the bottle)

blue surgical gloves
around the throat

like a new way
of breathing.

Communication Breakdown

We lay awake in the guest room
of my father's home.

Just back from Nine Inch Nails
at the Air Canada Centre.

Laying sweaty
above the sheets
north of Finch
at the DVP.

She is streaming footage from the show.
I am wondering what my father sees in this dragon lady
ten years his junior
who runs a string of massage parlours
in the city
and smells of cabbage.

I have a pretty good idea how they met
but don't say anything.

Now the missus is painting her toes
with purple glitter.

The air is stale
and depriving.

*You think some maniac will come in here
and behead us while we sleep?*
I ask.

*WHY THE HELL WOULD YOU SAY SOMETHING
LIKE THAT,*
she bellows.

I shrug my shoulders
and roll over.

Where I come from there are no windows,
only points of entry.

She will never understand.

Personal Touch

He said he could make a living as a hit man
and when I pointed out that he didn't even own a gun
he said he'd use a knife, give it his personal touch,
that three cuts to the sternum would be his signature
'cause everyone needs a signature
and he was right, the teller at the bank
always demanded a signature
gift card etiquette as well;
mine is more chicken scratch than signature,
slanting casually down
and to the
right.

Rubber Brown Curtains

The rubber brown curtains over the motel window,
heavy and domineering,
like day could be night just as well
with little imagination.

The tv on static
as if messages from god
never come from
free HBO.

Every surface
lazy deathbed
musty.

Perfect for country crooners
of a half century ago.

The pickers
and the drinkers.

Just the right amount of bone chill misery
and charm.

A toilet that works
if you learn to jiggle the handle
just right.

Many cold water showers
like entering the priesthood.

In an old industrial park
on the outskirts of city.

$45/ night.

Discount liquor
and discount women.

Like highschool dropouts
should have a place to continue
their schooling.

Even the phonebook
bolted down.

No bible
because there's no
point.

Nothing saved.
Not even coupons.

The rubber brown curtains for a reason.

Rubber, so nothing stains,
brown to mask the colour of dried blood
and/or vomit.

No one alive and kicking
before noon.

The ice storage
filled with dismembered feet
most the time.

The cops
knocking on doors
looking for some bus station runaway
named Trixie or Angel
or Trinity

or one of those other big screen names
the working girls lift from
the movies

nowadays.

Get Help, Not Food

He said his little sister was in recovery.

I asked him what for
and he said the needle.

I asked him if he got to visit her
and he said a couple times
a month.

Then I asked him what the food was like
and he winced
and I knew just what he meant.

At the age of 34
I was put in the madhouse
and fed nothing but a dry morsel of chicken
and a small scoop of potatoes
every day for a month.

Others chewed their bed sheets.
One lady was big on swallowing balled up paper from spiral
notepads.

Yet another commentary on the food,
I suppose.

Two Queens

are good to have
in poker
but not in life

and their meeting was televised
and they were nothing
and the pleasantries they exchanged
meant nothing

just two old ladies in diapers and sunhats
half-senile
smiling for the cameras

and when it was over
(the tea and biscuits
and such)

the world went on
as before

like it always
does.

Controlled Burn

First
they chopped off the head
with a hack saw
then the hands and feet
to make identification
difficult
then they pulled all the teeth
one by one
with a pair of pliers
and poured gasoline over the body
and set it alight.

In the bathtub
of a Brooklyn apartment.

All because he was five minutes late
to a meeting.

And you thought your boss
was tough.

Keep this in mind
the next time you get
written up.

Day Pass Diva

Released on day pass
he kept muttering to himself.

Something about monkeys in space
and complex carbohydrates.

I could see the admissions bracelet on his right arm
even though he wore long sleeves in summer.

The woman that was with him seemed quite distressed.

Rubbing his back to calm him
like dealing with a beached whale
or something.

Then I decided to have some fun.

Excuse me ma'am, but I think you dropped your wallet.
She looked down and sure enough she had.
When she bent down to pick it up
I leaned in close to the ear of the nut job
whispering that he was being watched
and we were all in
on it.

After that, it was complete fireworks.
As he ran around the store flailing his arms like he was on fire.

His woman trailing behind,
trying to make things better.

As he made his way through sundries
then general pet care.

Before getting into it
with some sales associate
in Womens lingerie
because she wouldn't open up the dressing room
so he could try a few things
on.

Summer High Season

Summer patios in full swing.
Everyone people watching with bags
of purchases between their feet.

It is the summer high season.
Dining tourists by the water.

There is much foot traffic.
Umbrellas over each table advertising popular stouts.
Everything on the menu hard to pronounce
and obscenely overpriced.

But no one seems to care.
Everyone wants to be seen.
It's a question of status.

The house wine comes out
and the whole table applauds
as if they have just watched
Mozart perform.

Instead of the skinny obnoxious waiter
for tips.

Topless Beach

Some men are trailblazers
and the rest
fill out cubicles of
mediocrity

and the little Asian man
who decided that everyone
should be topless
on a topless beach
was a trailblazer,
and if the people were not willing,
he would have to set
the example.

Taking a machete out of his satchel
he decapitated himself
right there under a yellow beach umbrella
that never once
wavered.

Everyone screaming,
still refusing to go
topless.

The cabana boys applying their many oils.
An area cordoned off by the local authorities.

The white sand beach
a little less so
now.

But everyone still refusing
to go topless.

Desperation is a Full Tank of Wanting

We are standing by the curbside
after LAX
outside a Del Taco in East Hollywood
with our dinner
when a car full of Chicanos bounces by
making a bunch of hand signals
before the skinny one hangs out the passenger side window
flicking his tongue rapidly
saying: yeah, *just what I like.*

The missus is disgusted.
I am concerned.

I want to give the poor boy my number
or someone else's number
or the number of someone who can help
from the sweaty jowls of the yellow pages
(some East LA baby mama hood rat with congenital herpes
and a nurturing way
perhaps),
so he can get what he's looking for
and lose his virginity finally
and stop circling the block

so low on
gas

and confidence

and
Life.

California Roll

The stop sign is there for effect.
No one in their right mind actually stops for it.
A California roll, at best,
like a lazy moment of silence
before the latest sports game.
Time is a sweaty armpit of loss
and the business of living trumps all—
the fuck finger and a fridge of beer
and late model lease-to-own cars backed into newly paved
driveways
with a healthy respect
for the act of
sodomy.

Strangling Parrots, Choking Chickens

The billowing green fog of lazy bird death chatter
hangs coat rack assured
over my receding hairline.

Temples enclosed
and throbbing.

As I poke at the electrical outlet
with the nob of my dick.
Working toward climax,
hoping to circumvent the electric
company.

To shoot these walls up full of a little juice.
Homemade is always best anyhow,
ask any health nut.

My orange palm tree boxers fallen away
like last minute ankle warmers.

You get desperate, start to wing it.
Everything on the fly.

It's criminal really— damn electric company.
Those bastards raised the rates again.
Third time in ten months.

Electricity is unaffordable for many now.
Everyone is looking for alternatives.

I hope this works.

First Day of School

Across the street from the school
a group of 10-12 children are dragging
their feet through the dirt
then along the pavement,
trying to scuff their new shoes.

It is the first day of school.
A time honoured tradition, of sorts.

The older boys waiting in the schoolyard
like a pack of hyenas.

For new shoes
and lunch money

then up against the chain link fence
for the coup de
gras.

Even the Strippers Making Change

There was a no fly zone.
A curfew as if everyone were fifteen again.

And people scurried about like small and terrible mice
on two legs.

Only coming out for a short time,
and only then for the necessities.

The newspapers full of fabrication and rumour.
A blackout for dramatic effect.

Even the strippers making change.

It seemed that everyone had lost their heads
but the mannequins in storefront windows.

They remained chalkboard calm
and I began to admire them for that
each time I passed.

On my way past the lithograph shop
full of signed limited edition
worst case scenarios.

The food truck taking all its condiments inside
like some rare and precious
jewels.

The abstinence lobby out front city hall
fucking like rabbits to make up for lost time.

So I could get a stick of bread from the Estonian bakers
two thirds on its way to
stale.

They Always like to Ask if You Are a Threat to the Community, but Never if the Community is a Threat to You

I like to circle by the nuthouse
every now and again
because nostalgia
is a bitch.

Then I swing by the grocery store along Princess
that is open 24 hours
because time should never
be a constraint.

Complex carbohydrates either.

Going aisle to aisle.
A basket under my arm as if I'm expecting.

Frozen foods
like winter come
early.

The stock boys all underpaid
and dark light broken home mother's basement
popping whitehead pizza face
malware computer geek
surly.

Standing in line
with my big dumb Buddha smile
like all the rest.

Beside the impulse buys.
The many Hollywood scandal rags
glossy gift card inviting.

Waiting for my turn at the cashier.
To make an impression that doesn't matter.

With a basket full of processed food
that will poison me
fast as anyone can say
uncle.

Fallout

A blue roadster
with blacked out windows
and the stereo pumping
speeds into the parking lot
with the passenger side door open
and without stopping
a large foot from the driver's side
kicks a blonde out of the car
and speeds off.

The woman slams her head
but does not seem to notice.

Jumping up
she chases the car a few feet
throws her purse at it
and yells:
ASSHOLE!

Then she begins to cry
head in hands.

The contents of her purse
laying in the road
like it all went
wrong.

Banana Boat Princess

The dancer
at the peelers
feeds my friend a line.

Some sorry puss story
about Castro,
the last raft out,
watching her father be tortured
with hot irons
as a little
girl.

I recognize her
from the call centre
I used to work
in.

She does not seem to
remember me.

As she works my friend over
for free drinks
and he follows suit.

Shoving a few extra dollars
down her thong

for her
troubles.

Real Estate is at a Premium

Cardboard condos
sprouting up everywhere.

The out of work and newly worked.

Intravenous drugs.
Sleeping bags of lice and circumstance.

Shopping carts
full of tin cans
and naked barbie dolls

with half the heads
missing.

Dinosaurs Are Extinct, and So Were We

Finishing each other's sentences is not always
a good thing.

Movie night, like the big boys
have the inside track on your cerebellum.

But things take time to figure out:
the mastery of steam power
the eight hour workday
a spice rack full of nothing
but Thyme.

And no one said anything
but we both seemed to know.

Things got very quiet.
Like mourners at a funeral.
Day after day.
Week after week.

Dirty undergarments no longer hidden.
The many jealousies and suspicions.
Dinosaurs are extinct, and so were we.

She doing her thing
and I doing mine
like two people living under
one roof

with a car that won't start

and all the rest of it
that never
stops.

For Another Minimum Wager

Work in under an hour.
Alarm clock tyranny realized.
There is no promise the car will start.
Yesterday is not today.
The yowling cat unfed.
Your cleanest dirty shirt will do.
All that diary has made you constipated.
So much effort that you see black spots.

Bent over the toilet
you push so hard
bones crack.

My Disarming Believable 5.75/hr Phone Voice

It was when I was dating this Jesus freak
in Letitia Heights
that was saving herself for the Nazarene
or the second coming like pizza night all over again
or years of therapy
like so many
before

while her Sunday choir roommate
(ironically named Faith)
let some slinky meek-shouldered bartender named Chad
handcuff her to the bed
each morning
and come upstairs for coffee
to laugh about it
and to brag to me
that women were less than pocket watches
without the time
and that she was waiting for him—
ass in the air—
just like the other three girls
he had on the side
who he'd promised
to marry.

A lesson in meat, he would tell me.
No action for me, of course.
I was a gentleman.
My friend Barkley picking me up from work
in the brown family shit box
after the Monday to Thursday
5 to 9.

Cold calling freezer orders of beef
20 hours a week

following the same script as the next fifty phones
beside me.

All with different sections
of the phonebook.

In a non-descript third floor loft
along Dunlop Street,
Barrie
so if the family of those taken ever wanted to firebomb
it would be difficult
to find.

And this was my life at seventeen.
Make the sale, no matter what the cost.

There was a commission
but you never heard
about it.

The supervisors
digging through your trashcan
after shift
looking for signs of
discontent.

Everyone Joe Stalin
smiling.

If you ever want a lesson
in the fundamental goodness
of Man
hustle recent widowers
with the early onset of dementia
out of their last few dollars
for $5.75/ hour

and drink away
the profits

in the evenings
that follow.

If there is
or ever was a god,
he is an asshole
of the highest
order.

And I am right there
beside him.

My seventeen year old self
following script
after script

after
script.

Fashion Week

in Milan
which means everyone
is dressed as a slimming
97 pound anorexic candle holder
in $500 stilettos.

You'd think it's a hunger strike
but it's not.

It's fashion.
That's what the pundits all tell us.
Cutting edge, like a brand new pair of scissors.

It is good that the human race
is so practical.

Now I understand.

Three mile Island
and fanny
packs.

DDT into the faces
of small children.

Celebs
taking to twitter
and dressing up as banana peels
at Cannes,
to give violence
the slip

because war is bad
like all those Japanese monster
movies

from the
1950s.

References

that may be a problem.

Two or more
you say,
at least one past
employer?

I sat through WHMIS,
that has to count
for something.

YES YES, the references,
I know.

Twiddling work world thumbs,
I know.

The throbbing blood blisters
and many calluses
never enough.

You want blood.
You need references.

Who
to speak up
for you

in a world
long gone

silent?

Memory is a Bitch

The boy went to school
down the alleyway
just like every other day
but that day
he never made it.

And 27 years after his disappearance
the fuzz wanted to pin it
on some guy from Massachusetts
who killed kids for
kicks.

They found a storage locker
less than a mile
from the alley where the child
disappeared
belonging to the suspect.

When they dug a few feet down
they found the teeth of four different children
but not the child in question.

When asked about the child's disappearance
by a court appointed forensic psychologist
the convict leaned in close to the glass
smiled
and said:

memory is a bitch.

He then knocked on the glass
asking that he be taken back to his cell.

Fluffing his pillow
on the top bunk
for his afternoon
nap.

His Rusted Out $200/as is Baby

He was trying to fix his car
so I suggested he not hold the choke open
with a dead rat
from the trap the night
before.

There was certain respect demanded.
Many music room doorstops
to be had.

If the thing was to be saved there should be some scrap of honour.
His rusted out $200/as is baby.
A lemon from the first.
The salesman in head-to-toe corduroy
assuring him it would be as loyal as any wife.
He wasn't lying.

The thing drove four blocks before it failed.
Mounted on cement blocks for many months after.

But this one was a believer.
Those black southern Baptist dancing end of days folks
would love him.

Like the healing highschool dropout hands
at least three women had forbade
to ever touch them again
could make the difference.

Day after day I did my part.
Turning the ignition
and giving it gas.

His eyes blazing with hope.

Each time
the engine kicked over

a few times
before stalling
again.

Not quite terminal cancer patient hopeless
but getting there.

Girls' Softball

like watching paint dry
without all the excitement
of paint

at the local park
as is the local custom

her parents
in the bleachers
raving on.

Like it's the world series.
Like cold fusion has been achieved.
Like the Nobel Prize for General Boredom has just been
handed out.

As their daughter throws some eater of cookie dough
on her period
trying to not bleed through the uniform
out at first,
some frumpy muffin top
who will stand over the photocopier
for the next forty years

thinking herself Apollo moon landing important,
demanding to be called an administrative assistant
and not a secretary,

messing up
the morning coffee
run

like ineptitude

never
retires.

Spiral Notebook

I remember looking at my spiral notebook
in class
and noticing how much its spirals
mimicked the milky way.

The way coloured chalk
and white chalk were kept apart
as if segregation never
ended.

How three quarters of students
wore grey on an overcast day
and vibrant colours when the sun
was out.

I began to see patterns everywhere.
Connections no one else could see.
Hyper-sensitive in such a way
that my fingers were always popular
with the ladies.

But I could still park a car.
Hold down a dead ender.
Cut myself shaving without breaking the bank
with panic…

Picasso
saw upside down noses
instead of the number seven
and made a career out of it,
but some folks are just
insane.

Empty Nester

Sitting
in a greasy spoon
in redneck
Canada.

Listening to some 50-something
empty nester
try to guilt trip her only
20-something son
into forsaking
college.

And I am reminded
on Norman Bates.

His love
for his mother.

As I eat my fries
in silence
two tables away,
with beef gravy
smothered all over the top
like the cows
of distant fields
are just happy

to be
there.

Crabs

Go to bed
with something
that says it
loves you.

Wake up
with crabs.

And I am fifteen
again.

Perched
over the porcelain
along Meadowland
Avenue.

The electric heater
on high.

Trying to figure out
if it was my mother or my father
this time.

Picking
those tiny black sons of bitches out
with my fingernails.

Watching them kick around in my hands
before flushing them down.

Everything slumber party
extramarital.

You can always expect blood
with anything

that
burrows.

Short, Bald, and Ugly

did not go over well
with the focus groups
who did not want to see themselves
(the misery of their lives)
any more than they had to,
so the new tv series
never got past the pilot
before all the actors were replaced
and all the scenes reshot—
everyone rich and beautiful
with a six pack
this time
spooning under sunsets at various beach locales
feeding each other strawberries
and cheesy lines,
and the focus groups said YES
and the money got on board too
and the networks saved a slot
in primetime
(as they
do)

so the short and bald
and ugly

would be home
to see
it.

With Mother's Day Just Around the Corner

She was almost sober
which was another way of saying
a little less in the bag.

Falling off the couch
with half melted bonbons
stuck to her underwear.

All his cigarettes smoked down
to the day soap filter.

And when he arrived home,
she was on him.

Like a hungry jaguar
she pounced,
there was no breathing room.

Did you finally get a job today,
she mocked,
did you even try?

Calling all the children into the kitchen
she continued:
everyone look at your father,
what a useless no good prick he is.
My mother warned me not to marry such a hopeless loser
but did I listen,
no!

The younger children cried.
The older ones knew better.

If there was to be dinner they would prepare it.
Bottles of milk to be boiled for the infants.
Everyone springing into action.
With Mother's Day just around the corner.

Then she slurred a few indiscernible words
marched into the bathroom
slammed the door behind her
and ran a bath.

Shoving the showerhead up her cunt
for the better part of
an hour.

Blue Wall of Sound

The cop pulls you over again
for doing 58
in a 55
and you want to
express the truth of it:

that he's fought with his wife recently over money
the Freudian implications of erectile dysfunction
seven o'clock shift change
with a weekly quota
to meet

but you smile a toothy smile instead,
produce your license and registration
thank the officer for his
time

adjusting your rear view for effect
putting your left indicator
on

watching bacon pull away
from the curb,
hoping the Mexican Mafia
has a hit out

not produced

by Phil
Spector.

Much Trouble Breathing

She lays down in bed
beside me
shoulders me awake
because I am having much
trouble breathing.

The heavy brown curtain
pulled aside.

The oscillating fan
afraid to commit.

As I sit up
blow my former self
into a tissue.

Think of many gravestones
tipped over
by the oily teenaged
white heads

of premature
ejaculation.

Brand Loyalty

The aging mob boss
could see well beyond the mountain of pasta
and sauce
in front of him
each night.

He knew he was a target
for some treacherous grease ball upstart
(likely from the rank and file)
looking to make a name for himself
just as he had once
done.

But they would need help.
The classic inside job.

So he summoned all the trusted capos
from the five boroughs
and made them all hungry goldfish
that forget to ever come up
for air.

And the bodies started turning up.
All blue in the face like there was only one colour left
in the crayon box.
And the nightly news could not keep up.
Heavy turnover in the tri-state area.

And then
everyone knew
what the aging mob boss
wanted them all
to know.

And the street dealers
went back to dealing
and the muscle

went back to muscling
in on turf

and no one ever again
questioned if the man at the top
was growing a little

boiled pasta
soft.

Gentlemen Prefer Blondes
that Swallow

The lumber yard
is full of wood,
the adult film industry
too.

And many young hopefuls
that want to make
it.

Waiting tables in the evening
along the sunset strip
because the casting couch blowjobs
that made Marilyn famous

haven't paid off
yet.

Winter Doughnuts

In the trunk of the car
you never see it coming.

The spinning parking lot car
doing winter doughnuts in the Anne Street plaza
after midnight
before the body work under your feet
bashes in a foot or so
after colliding with the other car
doing winter doughnuts
in the opposite
direction.

Everything goes quiet
and you imagine all sorts of things:
like everyone is dead
or the trunk won't open
and become suddenly cognizant
of the glaring lack
of oxygen.

And you think of the many mob rats before.
Taken for a drive for various indiscretions.
On the Mediterranean social club outs.

Of the many baseball bats and bone saws
that await you,
to make you disposable garbage bag
compactible.

And then the trunk opens after some minutes
and you play it Bogey cool
climbing out with an unlit cigarette in your mouth
and chatting up the girls.

And then the work begins.
The drunken brain trust under half a foot of snow.

Now tasked with trying to figure out a way to hide the damage
so the father of the driver of the car
can make it to work in the morning

in the family vehicle

without
noticing.

Grunt

I was a grunt
just like the rest.

Hauling lumber
up many stories
throwing my shoulder out
for a pittance
so summer townhouses
could be built
blazing starting block
sprinter fast.

And the foreman
could take his wife
to Jamaica.

And all the Jamaicans
could make rent
north of the
city.

As I handed them plywood.

Beside the preschool
where the children laughed and played
and pushed each other
on the swings,
not realizing that I was them
in fifteen
years.

With steel toe work boots
and no hope
at all.

Stand Up

The missus is downstairs.

Watching a comedy show
on late night television
where fat women make fun
of their weight
and Jews unload their many Holocaust jokes
like the moving company
banking coin on the big ticket items
for a comfortable tip
and the black man plays the race card
once again
like it's the only play
in the deck.

Outside
the garbage cans
that line the street
tip over.

Families of hungry raccoons
hit pay
dirt.

And I hear the missus laughing
every so often.

The many winged night things
buzzing against the window screen
wanting in.

As I forsake my better sense
yet again,
let the wine run freely down my gullet
like a long forgotten
river

and bleed all over
another page

of
living.

Last Call

He stumbled behind the work truck
parked on the street
in Brampton
and started retching
because it was good
form.

Perfectly good beer gone to waste.
Much of it bought on credit.
No one wants to see that.
Least of all your friends.

And so distance is the great equalizer.
Doubled over, with a mouth full
of vomit.

Separating from the pack.
Isolating his gimpy last leg
self.

The same way a dying dog
will crawl under the porch
to be alone

when it is
finished.

Sworn into Office, Now Swearing Under Oath

The voice on the television said this politician
from Italy or Spain (one of the Latin countries,
I do not remember which)
was embroiled in controversy.
It was claimed he had shown his ding dong
to some pretty little underage thing
at a party.
His wrinkled 78-year old nut sack
hanging there like a forgotten birdhouse
after nuclear fallout.
And his political opponents came out of the woodwork.
Women's groups asking for his head.
The girl's parents told the court she was traumatized,
I don't doubt it.

If some geriatric old bird
started pulling down her diaper
in the street
to show me her dried up old glory box—
now rabid porcupine
unkempt—
I wouldn't be able to sleep
for a week.

Bar Crawl

I followed the bar crawl
through cobblestone streets.

Getting louder and louder as they went.
The men with their many boasts and quarter-truths.
The many drunken girls stumbling cackle obnoxious
but somehow still pretty.

I was not going to the bar.
I could not afford to.

Walking home
in the rain
past the realtors
with the humming neon sun
 in front.

Ode to Herbert Spencer

The rainy day birds
on the lawn
picking off the worms
as they come up
out of the flooded earth
always make me think
of that night stalker Ritchie Ramirez
(what a naughty little soldier
that one
was),
the way he stood on
the other side of that kitchen island
and leveled his gun,
knowing curiosity would get
the better of her
and she would have
to look.

Coming up
to the surface
just like these many

rainy day
worms.

Twin Pit Bulls

The wind chimes rang incessantly.
Like dandruff had a soundtrack.

From the front stoop across the street
raving church choir
inviting.

And no one ever saw them.

Twin pit bulls
chewing through the fence line
each day the school children
came home.

Laughing
and playing their many hours
of tag
in the street.

Cowboys
and Indians,
no one ever wanting to be the Indians
and who could blame them?

The electrical box humming
for young girls to sit on
before the dildo.

Completely unaware
that locked jaws
were watching.

Something rabid
and off the chain
was eating its way closer
and closer

to the
bone.

Disaster Movie Narcissism

The airspace was closed.

The army called in to
restore order.

Tanks in the street.
Snipers taking up positions on neighbouring rooftops.
A negotiator brought in from the hill.
A state of emergency declared by the mayor's office.
A seven block radius evacuated.
Bulletproof vests handed out like poppies
on Remembrance
Day.

As I sat up in bed and yawned.
In orange droopy drawers with white palm trees.
The entire world at the ready.

Stirred awake by my own flatulence
like a backfiring car
under limited
warranty.

Stretch Marks Are Just Storylines that Carry On Too Long

Another wind storm
like downed trees
should be downed
lives.

The electrical outlet
always Geiger counter
threatening.

As I finish this bottle
and the bottle
after that

and write the ending
to the next great American
novel

on a napkin
from Denny's
(in 250 words
or less)

with as many folds
as any heavy set
woman.

There Was a Man

When I was nine years old
there was a man
going around the neighbourhood
trying to lure children
into his car with
candy.

Or at least
that's what they said
to keep you
afraid.

Over the PA system before each recess
with a repetition the advertisers
know so well
these days.

Each recess
my friend Darren and I
walked up to parked cars
and peered through the windows
but nothing ever
happened.

Looking back
I'm pretty sure it was all just
some late 80s ruse.

With the Reds losing steam
and the threat of hair metal
on its last legs

and no one left behind you
to push the swing
and make it into something dangerous
like AIDS
or the playground bully

or the PLO
on planes with no
intention of

ever
landing.

Forget Poverty, I Want to Know About the Nose Hairs of the Dinosaurs

The Ulysses S. Grant system
needs a serious overhaul.

No wonder the south is cotton pickin' mad.
Money siphoned away like life
from a willful infant.

Professors of this
and that.
From some of the finest institutions
in the land.

Spending taxpayers' dollars
so we can finally know how prehistoric man kept his hair
and why
according to the chronology
of early-Celtic hunting party
braiding.

I Have Found

the most honest one can get
is to drink yourself village idiot silly
and type,

to put yourself
in such a state that you
do not know what you are doing
or remember the least bit
of such business

the morning
after.

Let the sub-conscious
say what it will
unfiltered,
night after night
year after
year.

From the deepest darkest recesses
something approaching honesty
finally emerges.

Something
you would never say
if you ever tried to
say it.

**The Future Needs Rent Money
and the Cost of Diapers
Just like the Past**

We go to the tarot card reading
in the city
and what a surprise.

My lady could do so much better
even though I'm paying through the teeth
for the hustle.

To hear my chakras are misaligned
like un-rotated tires
after 30 thousand
miles

and a past love
will return
like thunder,

the back curtain of many mysteries
falling down
behind Madame Jasmine
of the crystal ball,
failing lazy close-pin
intermittently.

To expose
a crying child
sucking at the court ordered
milk tits.

And perhaps a few illegal immigrants
looking to learn the tricks of the trade
and bring their family over
and make a living

off Costco membership
unhappily married
new age soccer mom
stupidity.

Free Ride

The militarization of police, they complain,
like angry jocks that didn't get football scholarships
were ever kind to you.

Remember highschool?
I do.

I wore a necklace of dead animal parts
around my neck
and pretended to sleep in cemeteries
as a deterrent.

I knew I was never getting a free ride
and most of them were not either.

And that the majority would end up
angry entitled cops.

Now outfitted with assault rifles
and Kevlar vests
and all the latest shit
from the army
so the family dog
can be made into mince meat
with triple action hollow-points
as you kick in the family door
and enter.

A Bend in the Road is Worth Two by the Mistress

The window cleaners
of the 57th floor
are tired of office tower
pigeon:

removing beak
and smears
and feathers

off of glass
that looks like sky
while the Greek hotdog vendors
offer condiments
in the streets
below

and the traffic backs up
with much confusion

so the window cleaners can work illegally
up in the stratosphere,
hiring uncles and distant cousins
and brothers
alike

bringing most the family over
from El Salvador
and arming them with
squeegees

so the VP of operations
can bank his 800 grand/per annum,
bending his secretary over the desk
three times a week
to clean windows

just as the better business bureau
always intended.

My Week Beats Your Year

Whole phonebooks incinerated in less than a second.

People fashioned into ashtrays
by other people.

And then there's the personal holocaust of stomach acid
that shoots up my throat each night
burning away the esophagus.

The night sweats and the night terrors.
Blood out the ass like a backwards Vesuvius.

The head of my dying child
slowly eaten away by cancer;
necrotic and black and gaping,
the smell and the fluid
of that.

Packing the wounds for ten straight months.
Every traumatizing PTSD moment relived
with crystal clarity
forever.

The many shrinks and medications.
And of course, the bottle.

Feeling sorry for yourself?
Do not come around here with your many hard luck stories, my friend
the failed driving test
the one that got away
all that short on rent half empty fridge trying to be an artist
bullshit…

My week beats your year.
And all the years you might every live to see.

The weeping willows do not know how to cry.
I am fortified as any wine now.

I have no misgivings
about the ways
of the world.

All the horrors you can imagine
are a single thumbtack
to me.

Another 40 Year Man Goes the Way of Big Tobacco

He knew that equality was a lie.
That he was merely a cog in the machine.
Useful as a garbage bag.
Everything thrown away in the end.

But he had many children and grandchildren.
Kept working well into his seventies
because he had to.

And eventually he died
like everyone
dies.

And the family saved on funeral costs.
Chose cremation.

And the cheapest urn they could find
kept well clear of the kitchen
so grandpa Louie would not be confused
with the spice rack
come August long
weekend.

The grilled porterhouse
tasting a little
funny.

Bairros Africanos

Ever been to the favelas?

Me neither.
But it's a nice sounding word
as far as words go:

favelas.

Makes me think of falafel
made of people,
which is kind of what a favela is
if you think about
it.

Whole lives devoured
and digested
and shit back out
into the world
again.

Tow Trucks

along the shoulder
of the highway
like cynicism
on four
wheels.

As if things are going well
but they can't
forever.

The buzzards of humanity
CB radio

ambulance chaser
gathering.

Away Team

The cowbells rang out
in the final six minutes of the game
like the home team should mount one final
successful push to victory
against all odds
just like in the history books,
scoring in the final seconds
to great applause,
but they did not
and those too young to know rejection
froze on the spot
and the voice over the PA system asked for calm
and there were many fights
on the way back to parking
because winners should win
and losers should lose
and everything should always follow
a nice easy script
just like it does

in
Hollywood.

Bailiff

The bailiff liked to take people away.
And not in the same way that travel agents do.
And after work, he would unwind in the bar across the street.
Order doubles, play a few rounds of darts,
get good and drunk…

Then he would stumble home the whole seven blocks
to a fourth floor cold water bachelor.

To burn some toast and read the funnies
and pass out on a bed that 39 other men
had already died
in.

Paris in the Spring

Paris
in the spring,
the ladies love it;
fine wine
exquisite cuisine
and some underwear model named Jean-Paul
or Claude
that paints
and says your name
funny
when he's not going down
on you
and making motorboat noises,
doing that thing
with his tongue
that his wife
loves so
much.

Amen

A documentary film crew followed him
for many years.

The first paraplegic to ever climb Mt. Everest.

He was sold as a beacon of hope
to those physically challenged.

The war amps put up some serious coin.
There were many sponsors.

Apparently
the studio people were in talks
to make a mini-series about his life.

His early years being bullied for being different,
the many struggles he had to overcome.

A real inspiring
tear jerker
Netflix original.

But everything fell apart on the last day of filming.

When their Moses
of a few less below-zes—
this cripple of a billion nipples—
finally got to the top
looked out over the world
and pronounced:
well this wasn't worth it at all,
I may as well have stayed in bed
for the last three
years.

And that pissed everyone off
because it was the truth,

and no one likes the truth
when we're all trying so damn hard
to live a
lie.

Violence as a First Language

Violence is the language of prison
and the yard is where conversation happens.

Feuds, hits, drugs, trade in illicit contraband;
if there is going to be a problem, it will most likely
go down in the yard
and the guards know this.
There are some key indicators that there will be violence
such as a sudden rush to buy up things from the canteen.
Inmates stock up when they know the prison
will be in lockdown for a while,
so this sudden rush to the canteen will often tip guards off
that there will be violence…

But there is always violence;
must always be violence.

In one form or another.

Violence on the inside is like a conversation
on the outside:

conflicting views are posited,
arguments made,
and resolution.

Violence is the language of prison
and the yard is where all is understood.

The yard is where there is no confusion;
only clarity of intent.

A pure and total communication.

The yard is where everyone
comes together
and reputations are made
and lost.

Kind of like a schoolyard
for those
too big for the swings.

Except this yard
plays for keeps.

Slag

I always wanted a roommate, a cellmate,
no a roommate.

Someone on the outside
who could make calls from a payphone
without them being monitored
by Interpol
and there was Slag.

Metallic and forthright and obvious
sliding down the walls
into the water table.

The quiet type, like all men should be.
As if selective mutism is the unacknowledged virtue of…
oh oh, you almost got me pimping on Shelley,
his many Oxford protests
just the tired flaking dandruff of pomp
and privilege.

Silver spoons
and silver linings.

But not Slag, no no,
with his head in ovens of chance
and no chance at all.

Playing a losing hand, every hand.
Stolen cars in the chop shops
of circumstance.
Boots knocking together under grandfather clocks
that never tire.
Dumpsters full of dismembered femurs
in look the other way
hefty bags.

I see the flowers in bloom, yes yes…
The many yacht club pleasantries.

But that is not Slag.
And nothing that I know.

This is bloody biker bar knuckles.
This is summer solstice beheadings.

The failed composer
and the failed sex
drive.

The registered sex offender
birthday clown
making balloon animals out of
corner convenience
condoms.

The brute in the prize ring, at a third grade reading level,
with 39 ways to kill you
and not one of them kindness.
A sneaky left hook that comes out of nowhere.
The spit bucket full of blood and life and effort.
The ghost of Joe Louis practicing footwork
in front of the dressing room mirror.

And the dictionary is full of words
but LIFE can be full of meaning.

Just look at the able-bodied magic
that comes from the distended stomach lining
of baked bean hermaphrodites.

The storm cloud
and the storm troop.

Only the skeptics wanting either.
Mass graves just another I told you so.
Short on rent with the pacing landlord
of death.

But things can look up.
Not glass eyes, perhaps,
but many other tree top
things.

Take the mountaineer for instance
premature baldness
astrologists with gazing stardust
eyes.

But things must be measured,
it seems the standard classroom ruler is right
after all.

Not too high
not too low.

I don't like measured.
Neither does Slag.

My roomie, my flunky
of a thousand horrors.
The cursed tombs of the kings
like a creeping spider that crawls in your ear canal while you sleep
and dies.

Six on average if you are to believe the numbers.
But the numbers are fudged, even the calculator on the take.
The mayor is just the mob with a desk.
The beat cops receiving their envelopes at the first of every month.
The dancing girls passing along information and crabs
with equal vigour.
$9 drinks, like it has always been too expensive to suck air.
Local business extorted into bankruptcy.
The world series thrown again so the Indians can win something
in the span of their natural lives, that's nice.

An olive branch of nine innings played.
Game seven, the sporting game card hydra of as many heads.

And these are the many things we talked about.
Argued over, point by point,
syllable by syllable.

Increasingly inarticulate.
Waving arms with tidal starfish
competition.

Skunk drunk six nights a week.

Passing the bottle,
a thick miner's film
over the lip.

And he lived everywhere.
Never one to be confined.
In the stairwell
down the halls
in the pool shark's left
corner pocket.

All shots called
like the operator for
long distance.

Veggie gardens
on rusty east coast balconies
without water
choked dry and dumb
and dying
with exhaust.

A city of failing mufflers
and failed lives.

Drowning olives
in upscale date rape
martinis.

But not Slag, my roomie.

A mustache of dirt
and grass
clippings.

Making himself a liquid
which is not easy to do
when you have such broad
shoulders.

Pooling under the door
when you're 20 minutes into
a good nap.

Secret Santa

She
gave
him
crabs
and
it
wasn't
even
Christmas.

He
spent
a
small
fortune
on
all
the
necessary
creams.

Applying
them
daily
until
she

went
away.

217 Times

Forget to signal
and sometimes that
is enough.

Flagged down at the next light
a 52 year old spot welder
from Duluth
was dragged from his car
and stabbed in the face
and chest and legs

217 times
and left to
die.

I don't know what that says
about anything.

Maybe it says nothing
at all.

But it's a reminder
that not only crossword puzzles
will confound
you.

There is Stonehenge
and volleyball nets
too high for reaching.

And don't forget those vampires of Long Beach
all those years ago
that robbed the local blood bank
and were found up some alley
three blocks away
a few hours
later.

Injecting bread crumbs
into their arms
to soak up some of the mistake
they had made.

Patio Crowd

The summer patio crowd
always made me sick.

Trying to see and be seen,
as if the newly blind can circumvent
general impairment.

In muscle shirts
and short skirts
like puzzles without any
pieces.

Tourist dollars paying 75 cents extra
for cheese.

A pool of human vomit
spilling out into the streets.

A petting zoo
full of imbeciles
that all end up in bed
together.

They Are

they are cow prods into the aching heart of matrimony
they are city planning in the bedroom
they are high on blood thinners and low on gas
they are fingers through the hair of lazy pet shop tarantulas
they are a bookshelf full of blue rays
they are circumcision as performance art
they are start your own business before start your own life
they are roller skates along the boardwalk
they are cafeteria food tiresome
they are the last one picked for gym class
they are nuclear meltdown in a personal sense
they are divorce court, like those two opposing magnets in grade ten science class
they are skin tags on the imaginary backs of werewolves
they are Venetian blinds hung like Venetian men
they are basmati rice in white suburban cupboards
they are spinning green lawnmowers of absolutism
they are the seven signs of aging instead of the seven wonders of the world
they are a forest fire prevention pamphlet that is flammable
they are everything that comes out of the closet that is not gay
they are the lead story on the nightly news
they are 800 lbs shut ins cut out of their homes with unusually large scissors
they are M-theory, like the 13th letter of the alphabet sits at the front of the bus blue lunch pail retarded
they are life on other planets, so dumb it cannot stop coming here
they are coffee grinds in the family compost of the gainfully employed
they are the credit card people that will not stop calling
they are backed up sewers and backed up sex lives
they are conspiracy theorists, and crop circles, and skinny roach motel junkies
all in one

they are not like you
or me

or at least
not like
me.

Slow Cookers Are Only for Those with Time

I wish more things were sincere.
Like parking enforcement.
Those biddies get right to the point.

There is no slow building of momentum.
This is not meat brought up to temperature.
Tolstoy getting to the point after 981 pages
of bluster.

This is sudden death.
Where do you stand right now?

Either it works
or not.

No period of contemplation.
This is not a reflection pool.
Fuck Buddhism, I live and breathe
right now.

This is corner convenience
gun in your face
give me all your money
or you die.

So honest.
So pure.

What is said is meant.
Economy of verse.

The way it was meant
to be.

Everything
hopping wood chipper
final.

Easy as Pie

The real estate head
on the back on the bus stop billboard
promises to sell my home
easy as pie
satisfaction guaranteed.

It is prominent
and smiling
and assured.

Airbrushed
and youthful
looking twenty years
her junior.

There is no mention of commission.
Property taxes and transfer fees
and the like.

And don't forget all the other taxes.
The government never does.

Like a death sentence written into the culinary folds
of every dinner napkin.

But look at the view.
All the appliances stainless steel.

Accentuate the positive, I get that,
but at what point is it just lying?
Anything to make a sale.

Making my way through the McDonalds drive-thru
I am thwarted by a grey minivan
sitting in park.

There is just enough room to skirt by
if you mount the curb.

Pulling up beside the window
of the grey minivan blocking traffic
I slow down to look inside.

Some jiggling arm fat beluga
scaling no less than 500lbs
is knitting.

It looks to be a sweater
or the knit purl beginnings of Christmas slippers
in July
but I can't be sure.

She gives me the finger
like I'm in the wrong
and I drive off.

Thinking
this world is a strange
place.

Even without the sasquatch.

Ryan Quinn Flanagan is a happily unmarried proud father of none. Presently residing in the slowly dying mining town of Elliot Lake, Ontario, Canada with a large bear population that rifles through his garbage regularly. His work can be found both in print and online.

The author gratefully acknowledges the following publications
where some of these poems first appeared:

Asphodel Madness 2.0

Clutching at Straws

Leaf Garden Press

My Favorite Bullet

New Wave Vomit

Opium 2.0

Rose & Thorn Journal

Subtle Tea

The Camel Saloon

The Literary Burlesque

Toasted Cheese

ALSO AVAILABLE FROM
INTERIOR NOISE PRESS
www.interiornoisepress.com

INHERITANCE TAX
by **Jason Floyd Williams**
ISBN:978-0-9816606-0-8
Paperback $12.00 USD

DROUGHT RESISTANT STRAIN
by **Mather Schneider**
ISBN:978-0-9816606-1-5
Paperback $15.00 USD

GORILLA ARCHITECTURE
by **Carl Miller Daniels**
ISBN:978-0-9816606-2-2
Paperback $15.00 USD

MORE THAN THE ALLEY
by **Doug Draime**
ISBN:978-0-9816606-6-0
Paperback $15.00 USD

DISTURBING THE LIGHT
by **James Babbs**
ISBN:978-0-9816606-7-7
Paperback $15.00 USD

SOFISTICATED WHITE TRASH
by **J.J. Campbell**
ISBN:978-0-9816606-8-4
Paperback $15.00 USD

AN ELEPHANT HOLE
by **Justin Hyde**
ISBN: 978-0-9816606-3-9
Paperback $15.00 USD

BAD MUSTACHE
by **Glenn Hardin**
ISBN: 978-0-9816606-9-1
Paperback $15.00 USD

SALINE
by **Carl Miller Daniels**
ISBN:978-0-9816606-4-6
Paperback $15.00 USD

www.interiornoisepress.com

www.ingramcontent.com/pod-product-compliance
Lightning Source LLC
Chambersburg PA
CBHW020922090426
42736CB00010B/1008